A ROCKY LIFE

Things to consider

PIERRE LAFONTAINE

BALBOA.PRESS

A DIVISION OF HAY HOUSE

Balboa Press books may be ordered through booksellers or by contacting:

Balboa Press
A Division of Hay House
1663 Liberty Drive
Bloomington, IN 47403
www.balboapress.com
844-682-1282

Print information available on the last page.

ISBN: 978-1-9822-5241-0 (sc)
ISBN: 978-1-9822-5242-7 (e)

Balboa Press rev. date: 08/14/2020

CONTENTS

FOREWORD

From the very first time I met Pierre, I knew that we were bound to become good friends. Little did I know, back then in grade 7, that he would become a great friend that I consider family. We started hanging out when he invited me to his 13th birthday party and the first thing I noticed about Pierre was his charisma and awesome sense of humour. He realized soon enough that I love to laugh and he's the funniest person I know, so it was a friendship that was basically meant to be and that was built on laughter. The charismatic, outgoing and comedic sides of Pierre are what people see at first but that is only scratching the surface.

Pierre is intelligent, well spoken, courageous, passionate, resourceful and most of all he's a survivor! As you read Pierre's story, you will soon realize that it takes someone special to work as hard as Pierre has on his physical, emotional, intellectual and spiritual well-being. Having had long and deep conversations with Pierre has taught me to never give up, to be persistent while looking at the positive side of things by being grateful for the people and the memories that we cherish most. He has also taught me that there is no shame in stepping away or taking a step back from toxic people in our lives even, if sometimes, that is the most difficult thing to do. Pierre is one of the strongest people I know mentally and emotionally. When I say this, I'm not saying he's never broken down or has had awful days, weeks or months. I'm saying that through it all, he's always gotten back up. when a great deal of people would have been down for the count. His strength is shown through pure determination and the willingness to be better than he was yesterday and to show us that even though life hands you a shit hand, you can choose to be happy and you can choose love.

I believe that one story can change the world by helping one person at a time. Which creates a butterfly effect that has already helped me and that continues on helping me by making great memories and a whole lot of laughter but most of all by having meaningful conversations that make me want to grow as well. Pierre's story is one of growth and the pure will to survive. It takes a great deal of courage to write a story that makes one vulnerable, which is just another one of Pierre's great traits. He is an astonishing Father and Husband that is constantly working on self-growth. He has instinctively broken a cycle of abuse and to me that is spectacular! The world could use a great deal of «Pierres»!

All I can say is that I'm honoured to be part of Pierre's chosen family, he is a brother to me and I'm extremely proud of him. He's an example to me as I am certain he will be to you after you read his remarkable story.

Love you buddy,

John

PREFACE

Writing a book can be a daunting task. The author must ask himself a few things before he begins. The author must know who his target audience will be, and with that, make sure that he chooses words that will connect and relate to the reader. The author must be clear and precise when describing a scene or an idea, so the reader stays engaged and interested. The author must write from an open heart and not emphasize whether the book will be loved, well-received, or even become a best seller. Also, the author should choose his or her intentions for writing the book. Why is the book being written? Without purpose, the author can get lost by the book's potential and lose sight of why putting pen to paper is so important.

I have struggled to write this book for many reasons. I wanted to help people but often complicated things by focusing on the wrong things. Instead of focusing on my intention, I would focus on the potential fame and fortune a best seller could bring, often sabotaging my progress. By daydreaming of the novel's potential, I often found more significance in my daydreaming than the novel's actual writing. This daydreaming would eventually lead to a halt of progression because I would get trapped living the life I wanted, in my head, and not pursuing it into reality.

Instead of writing from the heart, I would appease to the reader, which made me feel pompous or unauthentic. These feelings would discourage me even further because I knew that I wasn't "keeping it real." I wasn't connected to my intentions for writing the book, which caused me to lose interest in the writing process. To be honest, another reason for experiencing such difficulties when attempting to write a book is that I can be lazy or tend to procrastinate. My laziness often disguised itself as the pursuit of perfection, and I was of the school of thought that "If I couldn't do it right the first time, I wouldn't even try." To simplify things, the primary reason for my lack of success was…ME!!! That's right, ME! I was to blame for my lack of motivation, desire to coast through life and poor work ethic. Often blaming outside sources for my lack of success, I came to the realization that I was solely responsible for my life's success. I realized that my success was totally up to me, and if I wanted to be successful, I would have to make better decisions.

Additional things that hindered my success were lingering thoughts. Thoughts like: "What are my parents going to think?" or "Will they continue to love me if I write the book?" or even "Will they continue to love me if my book is a hit and I outgrow them as a result?" My parents often mentioned that I should write a book about my life. I always felt like they weren't entirely honest and supportive when it came to writing my book. It's like they felt obligated to tell me to pursue my book because that's what good parents should do. I also felt like they could tell me to "write the book" because deep down, they knew that I wouldn't. The reason was simple; I was very loyal to them, even after my Father was arrested, convicted and sent to prison!! I was always there, helping them with projects around the house. I felt responsible for my Father going to jail, so I doubled down when it came to helping them! Even if that meant working like a dog for free! I would do it, no questions asked! I was like that because I worried about becoming successful and worried about stepping out from under my parents' shadow. Their reputation was damaged when the abuse that went on in our house went public. So I thought, "If I stay small, I won't bring any more attention to our family, and maybe they'll love me." Shame can be a nasty feeling, and it was tricking me into believing false narratives about who I was and about who they were! Even if they were abusive and toxic to my mental health and wellness, shame blinded me to things I knew were off.

Over the years, I have written many things such as poetry, songs and even began a fictional novel or two. I also wrote a blog about my life, which my parents did not approve of, which wasn't a big surprise. I stopped writing when I reconnected with my parents. After we patched things up, nothing seemed to get me fired up to the point where I could not drop the pen. I felt small again, and I would write for a while, but never felt like I had any direction. Worried about what they might think, I needed to find a way to organize my thoughts to avoid being all over the map. I had not yet felt like the late Dr. Wayne Dyer when he said that he was being guided towards writing his novels. Like some external force was pouring through him, guiding him to write his masterpieces!! Up to that point, I had a few flashes, but nothing to the extent of what he experienced. My hands never felt cramped because of all the writing. However, lately, I have been feeling a sense of urgency, like I'm being drawn to pen and paper, eager to share my experience and how I inevitably saved myself. I feel as though I am being encouraged by a divine source to write my story. The truth is, I have had this story in me for a while, but my fear of sharing it was overwhelming. I always thought the timing wasn't right or that nobody would want to read my story. I feared the embarrassment that would come from people reading my story. I feared failing and worried about being seen as a failure. I also feared what my parents might think. One day, I realized that I would rather fail at something I was passionate about as opposed to succeeding at something I wasn't. I needed to forget about the potential haters!! We all have experienced fear at some point in our lives. Most people live in fear and die being fearful, and I am no exception. Most of us live our lives, making a living but never creating an experience for ourselves. We get caught up caring what others might think, so we follow the herd of mediocrity. Then one compromise becomes two, and then our dreams become distant memories, all because we lacked the courage to push through our fears.

I realized that I did not have a big enough "why" for writing my story. I needed to figure out why I wanted to write this book! Because without direction, I was planning to fail! It's imperative for all of us to find our "why" when we want to do what we want to do. One of my "whys" is that I want to help people transform their lives. I want to help them transition from Victim to Survivor and then again to Thriver!! Another one of my "whys" is desperation. That's right! DESPERATION!!! Can a person motivated by desperation accomplish great things? Of course!!! Some of the most significant accomplishments in the world have come from a state of despair or the feeling of being backed into a corner.

Here's a quote from Napoleon Hill's Think and Grow Rich that will further explain what I mean:

"A long while ago, a great warrior faced a situation which made it necessary for him to make a decision that ensured his success on the battlefield. He was about to send his armies against a powerful foe, whose men outnumbered his own. He loaded his soldiers in the boats, sailed to the enemy's country, unloaded soldiers and equipment, then gave the order to burn the ships that had carried them. Addressing his men before the first battle, he said, "you see the boats going up in smoke. That means we cannot leave these shores alive unless we win. We now have no choice. We win or we perish." They won. Every person who wins in any undertaking must be willing to burn his ships and cut all sources of retreat. Only by doing so can one be sure of maintaining that state of mind known as a burning desire to win, essential to success."

As I write this book, I am 39 years old. My Wife and I have been forced to leave our jobs because of the Covid-19 pandemic, which has us in quarantine most days, with loads of free time. We are still bouncing back from a bad real estate investment that nearly bankrupted us. To add insult to injury, the Corona Virus forced a countrywide shutdown, slowing our financial recovery. With all this time and uncertainty upon us, my Wife and I decided that we would put our heads together to form a Super-group!! We are very interested in helping people but not in the traditional 9-5 environment that a job brings. Don't get me wrong, I'll get a job to pay the bills, but the thought of making someone else's vision come to life, through paid work, really depresses the hell out of me. I've been there, done that without much to show for it. It is this desperation that fuels me into wanting to leave my mark. I want to accomplish something bigger than I am!! Something that will help the masses live a life worth living and I must "burn my boats" if I am going to accomplish this or anything else I take on in the future.

I want to live a life with intention and purpose, which is another one of my "whys" for writing this book. I'm through living my life on autopilot!! Most people will live their entire lives on autopilot! Never pursuing goals or following their dreams, they go through life's daily hustle and bustle without smelling the roses!! Looking for our next instant fix of dopamine, we wander the planet like zombies, without any intention or purpose. We all want to be big stars, but rarely do we want to put in the necessary work and time required to get there. We often feel lost!! Searching for the meaning of life without knowing what it means, we fill our internal voids with external things or stimulants never seeming fulfilled. I know that I need to make changes to break my autopilot cycle. This book is one of those changes!!

I read Viktor Frankl's Man's Search for Meaning, and this quote helps sum this up for me:

"Man does not simply exist but always decides what his existence will be, what he will become the next moment. By the same token, every human being has the freedom to change at any instant."

Changing has often been compared to a snake shedding its skin. The significant difference between snakes and humans is this: snakes shed their skin when they're ready to grow as opposed to humans who change when they want to grow. We don't wait until we are ready to grow or change! If we waited until we were ready, we would never change at all!! Instead, what we do is force ourselves to grow!! We pull and rip off our unwanted skin to grow, which is why changing is difficult, challenging and often painful! Even as I re-edit this book, I make changes. The story of your life will always change because you change. The story I started writing three years ago has changed because my perspective of it has changed. I don't think like I did three years ago because things in my life have changed!

What I am about to share with you is what I do in regards to striving for a better life. I picked up these tricks and hacks while on my journey of healing and have adapted them to my own life. Now, I want to be clear when I say that this is my blueprint for success, and it may or may not work for you. What I want you to do is simple, take this information with a grain of salt! Everybody and their dog has an opinion on how to live the best life!! I don't want to pretend that I know how you should live your life!! I'm not that guy!! Besides, I don't think there is one way to strive towards living a great life but many ways to live a great life. The bottom line is this: feel free to adapt anything you read in this book towards your own life and disregard everything else. The definition of insanity is doing the same thing over and over again, expecting a different result!! Having said this, if what you've been doing isn't working for you, please consider this information with an open heart!!

There will always be problems present in your life... always!! Just as you get through a problem, it seems like there's another one right there waiting for you to tackle, get through or get defeated by. If you want to get through and address these problems, you must be open to continuous development and growth. You must work on your resiliency!

It's like Rocky Balboa said:
"It ain't about how hard you hit, it's about how hard you can get hit and keep moving forward."

You must dedicate the time needed to develop yourself, away from everyday distractions. It is with this dedication towards your growth that you will become more confident in your abilities. If you can't incorporate continuous growth within your lifestyle, you'll have to consider being defeated often, which will undoubtedly wear heavy on your soul, spirit or essence. I give you the same advice I am striving towards right now, even as I write this book. I'm just like you!! I want to be better and also want you to be better... whatever that looks like for you.

Focus on what you want to achieve, do what it takes to

get there and leave as many distractions behind you! If you want an easy life, you must be ready to make hard decisions. Those who take and make easy decisions usually end up living a hard life. We see this with the obesity epidemic ravaging the Western World!! In general, those who are obese are making easy decisions. It's pretty easy to become overweight!! Just say yes to the extra slice of pizza or cake, skip being active altogether, and over time, you'll pack on those extra unwanted pounds! It's much more challenging to stay fit and healthy nowadays! You have to be active while eating healthy consistently, and that takes discipline!! Again, those who choose easier decisions will eventually live a hard life! That's because they are unwilling to take the hits and move forward, they're not even willing to get in the ring! So, get in the ring of life!! Take the hard hits!! Get up and use them as learning opportunities! Then, adapt your approach so that you can gradually become better!

Another thing to consider!! You are the creator of your own life! The main actor in your movie if you will. You are the only one who can decide whether your film will be a blockbuster or end up in those bargain bins we often see in Dollar Stores!! With that being said, part of making the hard decisions towards living a carefree life is, you'll have to stop listening to the cynical critic within yourself. The voice that tells you, "you'll never make it; you're not good enough" or "you don't have enough education." Happening to most of us, the voice in our head stops us from doing the right thing or pursuing a fantastic opportunity because of our limiting beliefs.

I'm giving you permission to tell that voice to shut up! My inner voice had me believe that I could not write a book because I wasn't qualified enough or because I wasn't educated enough. The voice convinced me that nobody would read my story because nobody cared! This inner voice even dared to tell me that I wasn't good enough!! Imagine that! Finally, I took it upon myself to tell that little insecure voice inside me to "Shut the fuck up!" "I got this!" It took time, but here I am with you as you read this book!! You must empower yourself!! You must stand up within yourself and stop living in the basement of your soul!!

Our stories can be like tools and, if used correctly, define who we are and where we are going as individuals. However, if used in the victim state, our stories hinder us. They keep us down or in a state of fear. They keep perpetuating a feeling of "poor me" and a general sense of defeat! Having said this, we can use our stories to empower ourselves and the people around us. Our stories are tales of courage and strength! They describe our resilience and compassion! They talk about our unshakable desire to persevere and move forward! They talk about how people can pull themselves out of the pits of hell to find their version of heaven!

That being said, I hope that you'll enjoy this book and the content within. I hope this book helps you get your ass in gear! I hope this book helps you move towards your better self, your true self. I wish you growth, prosperity and the willingness to take your life in hand because, we only have one!

With Love,

Pierre Lafontaine

CHAPTER 1

THE CHILL OF DECEMBER

Disclaimer: before you read this, be aware that I will describe the sexual abuse I experienced as a child in detail. I don't want anybody else to experience what I've gone through as I know the damages abuse can cause. It has taken me years to climb out of the hole I dug for myself, and I wouldn't wish it upon my worst enemy. The intention of sharing my story is simple: context. Without context, it might be difficult to understand my perspective. I hope you read this with an open heart.

It's early December, and it's my Mother's birthday. We have been celebrating at my Aunt and Uncle's place who live nearby, and as we were on our way back home, I remember my Mother being drunk. She had one or two drinks too many and was intoxicated in the passenger's seat speaking gibberish. My Father was driving us home and, in his usual comedic ways, was playfully teasing my Mother for being intoxicated. My Brother and I thought this was funny, so we joined in on this innocent fun. I don't know if my Father was drunk, but if he was, he was keeping it together better

1

than she was. One thing I know for sure, he had been drinking. Once we got home, we all went to bed. At the time, my Brother and I shared a bedroom and even slept in the same bed. My Father put my Mother to bed and then joined us in ours for some midnight roughhousing, then we all fell asleep.

It's after midnight, and I am woken up by something that I have not experienced before. I'm lying in bed, and my Father is wedged between my Brother and I. I'm in a half-asleep, half-awake state of mind, and I remember my Father using my hand to masturbate himself with. I remember being still. I wasn't afraid if anything, I was curious. As I tried to figure out what was happening and why my Father was doing this, time seemed to slow down. The event probably lasted less than 5 minutes, but it seemed to go on forever. I was between the ages of 8-9 years old, so I knew nothing of masturbation and or sexual abuse. This was something new, something I was experiencing for the first time, and because I loved my Father, I didn't question what was happening. I pretended to be asleep and then rolled over. As a matter of fact, I don't even think he knew that I was awake.

After I rolled over, he went to his bed, and I remember smelling my hand to see what his penis would smell like. Again, I was more curious than anything. I did not feel angry or sad! Those feelings would come later on in life after I realized that he was abusing me. In fact, I remember being intrigued by my Father's penis. Remember, I was 8-9 years old, and my junk looked nothing like his junk. To top it off, my Father was my hero! He was a legend in my eyes, and I wished that my penis could be as big as his when I got older. The next day, I remember not overthinking the event that happened, and life went on as usual, given the circumstances. I never forgot what happened, but I was too busy being a kid. Plus, my morning cartoons and toys were much more stimulating than what my Dad did to me the night before. Honestly, I think my innocence didn't allow me to fully understand the severity of what had happened to me, so life went on.

It's been approximately a year and a half since the first incident. The memories of that night still lingered inside my brain, but somehow, I had reached a certain level of inner peace. I guess I thought that it was an isolated incident, a one time deal. I remember being about 9-10 years old, and my Father had organized a weekend for us and some relatives to stay at a friend's cottage, which was located on a lake. The cabin was old and needed some well overdue updates, it has since been torn down. Even HGTV's Elite Builders would have probably burnt it to the ground. It had huge spiders in it, the kind that make your skin crawl! Mice were also overrunning it! I remember thinking that I preferred the mice over the spiders because, at the time, I hated spiders. There were two bedrooms, one with a queen-size bed and the other had bunk beds. My Aunt and Uncle stayed in one bedroom while my Father, Brother and I shared the bunk beds.

We fished, explored, swam and made campfires!! We did all the typical things one could expect from a traditional camping trip. I remember sharing the bottom bunk with my Father as my Brother slept on the top. Once again, during the wee hours of the morning, I'm awakened to a familiar motion, and it was like I was experiencing a moment of Déjà Vu. Once again, my Father was repeating the same thing, but this time I knew what was happening. I had experienced it before, and yet, I was still in shock. I kept wondering why he was doing this to me. What was his purpose? All of a sudden!! He ejaculated all over my hand!! I froze! Like a mannequin in a department store, my body was stiff with disgust! As if nothing happened, he got up to clean himself while leaving my hand covered in his semen. Then, he came back, rolled me over and without missing a beat, went to bed. I, however, still had a handful of his semen in and all over my hand. It took me a while, but eventually, I fell back to sleep.

I was confused because I thought he peed on me! I wasn't very old and didn't know precisely how the human body worked, so I didn't understand what the substance was. I was just a kid! All I kept thinking was that I had never felt pee like this before! Sticky to the touch, I thought, "this can't be pee?!" I woke up in the morning, and as we were being called to breakfast, I made sure to state that I was going to wash my hands in the lake. Reliving the incident in my head, I scrubbed my hands clean. Until that point in my life, I had never used so much soap to wash my hands before!! I thought to myself, "This is fucken gross! Whatever this is, it's fucken gross!!" It reminded me of the movie Ghostbusters, when Bill Murray's character, Peter

Venkman, scoops the slime off of the library's filing cabinet! Pure grossness!

When I think about these moments, I can't help but feel anger towards my Father. I mean, can you blame me? How could he do that to me? I was just a child!! This triggers me a lot because, I think about my Daughter, who is ten years old at the moment and I could never do something so horrible to her...NEVER!! As I think back, when my Father was arrested, I did not mention these two incidents to the Police who questioned me. I did this to avoid hurting him because I loved him. I didn't want him to lose everything and go to prison; I only wanted him to stop. I wanted us to remain a family so, I only spoke of the abuse that happened during my teens as I thought there would be enough evidence on him. Besides, I knew some of my friends had come forward to testify against him because of the events that happened during a Xmas Party. I'll get to that later. The Police who questioned me made it sound like they were there to help my Father, so I spilled my beans. I told them everything that happened to me and told them everything that I was aware of the night of the infamous Xmas Party. These Police Officers were kind to me even if they were about to unravel my whole world.

I remember not wanting to be interrogated on film as I feared the possibility of my Father seeing the video, so I suggested an audio recording instead, which they agreed to entertain. Talk about an experience! I had never imagined that I would be asked to testify against my Father, and a small part of me didn't want to. I think I was experiencing

Stockholm Syndrome. I felt terrible for my Father and almost sympathized with him. I had been so used to the abuse that it was part of my routine, I identified with it. I am so grateful that I found the courage to tell my story as it would be the first time that I did! Who knows who I would be if I hadn't been truthful. Some compromises should never be considered when it comes to your soul's health. We are often presented with events in our lives that challenge us to go one way or another. One way benefits you and your growth while the other does the opposite and destroys your self-worth. Up to that point, I had chosen to ruin my self-esteem for several years, but at that moment, in the interrogation room, I chose differently. I am still working on rebuilding my self-worth, so imagine how far down I would be in my rabbit hole if I remained silent.

So imagine this! You are woken up early on a Saturday morning by your Mother, who seems out of sorts, who tells you that your Father has been arrested for sexual assault. She is in disbelief and talks about how the accusers are liars and makes it sound like this will all blow over. While this is happening, you know the truth and know that shit is about to hit the fan big time!! I remember my Mother asking me if I knew what was going on because the Police wanted to question me separately.

We were standing in our kitchen, and I remember grabbing my Mother's shoulders while saying, "Hold on, cause this is going to be a bumpy ride!" She tried to probe me for additional answers, but all I said was, "Wait until I am done with my statement! We'll talk about it after I come back home." She was reluctant to yield but did so anyways. After being interviewed, I was brought to my house to meet up with my Brother and Mother, who showed up sometime after me. At the Police Station, my Mother was given access to my statement. When she came home, I was in the kitchen, and she met me there, tears flowing. She hugged me and told me she was sorry. I didn't understand why she was sorry but assumed it was because she felt like she hadn't protected me.

Years later, I would learn that this wasn't the first time my Father had been accused of similar actions and that maybe that's why my Mother was sorry back then. Perhaps she felt guilty!! In the kitchen, my Mother was next to me, and my Brother was next to her. He didn't say much until my Mother asked him to get closer, but he wouldn't. He didn't believe me and said that I was a liar. Unfortunately, that really hurt me and would not be the last time someone would accuse me of lying. An Aunt on my Father's side said that I was lying because my Father wouldn't buy me a car! Imagine that! I made up this elaborate lie for a car of all things!!

Before I continue, I think it's essential that you all know that even if my Father sexually abused me, I have forgiven him for his actions. I forgave him his sins as I want to build a better relationship, not with him but with myself. It's taken me years to learn that forgiveness is not meant to release the perpetrator of his burdens but, in fact, to free yourself from yours. It's important for you to know this because my intentions come from my heart, and I am not in the game of bashing my Father. I want to lean towards the positive and not the negative. I am writing this without judging him or casting him in a bad light, even though he has put himself in less than favourable situations on several occasions. I have to realize that I don't own his decisions!

I have spent many years tearing him down in my mind, which only fuelled my inner chaos and suffering, and I don't want that anymore, I want to be free! It's important to mention that my Father was also subjected to sexual abuse from his Father. It's like the school bully who picks on kids during recess to make himself feel better about what is happening at home. An Aunt of mine once said something in front of the whole family that stuck with me. I'm going to share that with you now. We were all gathered and talking about my Father and the situation he put us in. There were Aunts, Uncles, Cousins and family friends there, and some were saying distasteful words about my Father without considering our (my Brother, Mother and I) feelings. They didn't mean to because they were simply caught up in a moment.

That's when she spoke up to say the words that would be forever ingrained in my heart. She said, **"Hate the sin, not the sinner!"** At that moment, time seemed to slow down as everybody paused to think about her words and maybe consider their own. At least, it seemed that way! I know it did for me! She might not know this, but those words triggered a process in me that would eventually lead me towards forgiving my Father. Even as I write this now, I forgive myself for the pain and suffering I put myself through, long after the abuse was over and done.

Speaking of forgiveness, it's important you know that I have chosen to remove myself from the toxic behaviour that my parents continue to exhibit. Just because I have forgiven them doesn't mean that we are best friends. What can I say? Being around them just feels weird! I know too much and refuse to maintain their illusion. I know about the lies and attempts made towards sweeping it all under the carpet. I know of my Father's escapades with other men even before he abused me, and I simply cannot allow myself to pretend nothing happened. I am the only one who chooses not to maintain their status quo, which creates conflict for our family and conflict for myself. In addition, they have decided not to acknowledge any issues but would rather pretend they never happened. Unfortunately, this triggers me in so many subtle ways that being with them feels unnatural and forced. Besides, I deserve to value my self-worth, and for some reason, when I am with them, I don't! I go into "little boy mode," where I care more about them than myself. I choose silence when I should speak up and choose kindness when I should be blunt. It's the little things that get to me. Instead of voicing my concerns, I remain quite while reaching for another beer. It doesn't feel good knowing they choose to ignore what has happened. It hurts to know that my Mother has chosen to stay with my Father even after all that has happened over the years. To be blunt, it's an abusive relationship, and I am worth much more than that. To continue to be exposed to them while expecting a different result is the definition of insanity!!

CHAPTER 2

LIVING A DOUBLE LIFE;
THE WORST PARTY EVER!

Overall, my childhood was decent! I say this partially because it's true and because every family has its own version of normal. For every family, what happens behind closed doors is considered the norm, even if seen from the outside world as being toxic. You get so used to living a double life, within the norms of your family, that you often can't see or register the toxicity happening right in front of your face.

An abuser often lives a double life to mask who they really are and what's really going on behind closed doors. They constantly juggle their inner and outer worlds while hoping the two never collide. They manipulate others around them to get what they want and often use guilt to accomplish this. What people sometimes forget is that the victim of abuse also lives a double life. Often using the same tactics as their abuser, their goal is simple: don't tell anyone! I didn't want anyone to find out about my secret because I feared being ridiculed or ostracized. Being straight, I didn't want people to think that I was gay. I knew that there would be financial consequences if it all went public and didn't want to pain my Mother and Brother with my problems.

In a way, I was like Jim Carrey's character, Stanley Ipkiss, from the movie "The Mask." I got really good at being a Joker while keeping my lies straight in the background. I had friends but never really trusted them enough to open up. I feared intimacy with girls because I was conflicted about my sexuality. I ended up keeping a secret that wasn't mine to keep, which caused me to grow up faster than most people my age. OK, maybe not exactly like Stanley Ipkiss, but almost!

We lived in Canada. We camped, fished, played in the woods, went on vacations, visited family and celebrated all the traditional Catholic holidays. We did what typical Catholic families did at the time, in our area. We played outside without supervision, with sticks and make-shift tree-houses we built ourselves, mostly until dark. We biked around without helmets and ate what we thought was healthy at the time. We were part of the generation that was introduced to the ever-growing industry of video games, and yet, we still managed to get bruises and scrapes from jumping off make-shift ramps with our bikes.

Now, kids have video games for breakfast, which seems to have caused an overall desensitization towards people and our everyday reality. With readily available games that promote violence and war, it's no wonder that today's youth seem disconnected, almost like modern-day zombies.

In the winter, we tobogganed down hills way too steep, dug tunnels, and built igloos in colossal snow piles, never having any of them collapse on us. We drove snowmobiles way too powerful for our little arms to handle, and yet, we did so without killing ourselves. Imagine that! We lived in a time with less fear, where we didn't worry about ticks and obesity, and the term "offended" wasn't a trend.

My Father was a Police Officer, and my Mother juggled being a Home Maker while working a variety of Clerical positions. We lived in a small community. The kind where everyone knows your name. My parents were well-known in town due to their outgoing personalities and were both members of bands and often performed in the area. My Father even hosted a popular Folk Festival in our town during its early years. What I'm getting at here is that my parents were well known and liked by many people and to some degree, they still are despite what happened all those years ago.

OK, so now that you understand how well they were connected within our community, you might get a sense of what it felt like when the abuse went public. Before I get into that, let me give you an approximate time frame when it all started, to provide you with context. I've already told you about the first two incidents were I was abused as a child, but the abuse became a recurring event when I became a teenager, right around when puberty hit. The abuse was, for the most part, a daily routine. If not daily, every second day, for sure! The abuse consisted of masturbating together, where we often raced to see who would ejaculate first. My

Father also liked having me masturbate while showering. It turned into a game for us.

Again, I was conditioned into believing that this was normal and healthy even if, deep down, I knew otherwise. I want to believe that my parents always did the best they could, given their upbringing and circumstances. My Father's Father was, by today's standards, an alcoholic, and he and my Grandmother had my Father when they were in their forties. Having a few children before my Father, they attempted to manage a farm while my Grandfather worked outside of the home to earn extra money during Winters. I can just imagine how challenging it would have been back then!!

On a consistent basis, the abuse I endured started when I was in eighth grade and lasted the better part of my high school years. One Winter evening, during my Father's staff party, which was hosted at our house, it all came to a crashing halt. I had three friends over during this party, and we had fun with the Police Service's Hierarchy. Everyone was having drinks that night, and my friends and I had our own secret stash of beverages in the basement before joining the party. It was a pretty liberal party, so we continued to have drinks with our town's finest community members upstairs even if we were underage.

As the party ended, my friends and I slept in the basement. I shared my bed with one of my friends while the other two shared a separate bedroom at the other end of the basement. In a drunken stupor, I was awakened by whispering voices in my room. It was the familiar rhetoric my

Father often used on me, but this time, he wasn't speaking to me, he was talking to my friend. I was so used to hearing those keywords and phrases that I knew exactly what was happening at that moment. I was furious, upset and hurt! My Father was assaulting my friend while I was passed out in the same bed!! It was the first time I would come to realize that I wasn't the only victim. I remember getting up, making an attempt at sobering up and geared myself for a confrontation! I was pissed! If I could have turned green like the Incredible Hulk, I would have. I aggressively asked him what the hell he was doing, even if I knew what he was doing.

Until that point, nobody knew of our dirty little secret, and I wasn't too sure how to react. I felt used by my Father but also was worried about what my friend would think. My friend, although in a sick and twisted way, was being given a crash course on how my life had been going so far!! How would he react to all of this? Would he be scarred for life? Or would he tell everyone at school to ridicule me in a feeble attempt at revenge? I didn't know what was going to happen so I reacted the best way I could given the circumstances, I turned on my Father. A teenager almost always chooses his friends over his parents, and this time was no different! I had accepted that my Father was hurting me, through the abuse, but hurt my friend?! That hit me below the belt!! I felt gutted! After yelling at my Father to go upstairs, I could see the look on his face. He had a guilty look that screamed: "Uh! Oh! I've been caught!" The look on his face was the same a child would make having been caught with his hand in the cookie jar! It was almost playful! Which infuriated me even further! It might have been a game before that night, but now, that there were more players, the gloves were off!!

We continued our confrontation outside my room. My Father was drunk, and more or less played it off like it wasn't a big deal. I remember telling him to: "Get the hell out of here and go to bed!" I was so angry that it empowered me. It was the first time I would feel furious towards my Father, and I swear I felt invincible. He tried reasoning with me for some reason, so I grabbed a chair and violently through it up against a wall. It crashed so hard that one of the steel legs bent. I'm surprised my Mother didn't wake up. I wanted to kill him that night, and if I hadn't thought of my friends, I probably would have tried! I could handle being abused because I was used to it, but to do it to my friend?! I was beside myself with anger and sadness all at once!! Sadly, this would not be the only time my Father and I would experience physical altercations. A child should never have to fight their parent. Unfortunately, I would not be afforded such a luxury!!

Having seen what my Father was capable of, I started wondering if there were other victims. As the years passed, I suspected other victims remained in the shadows, probably never to be heard from. I can't prove this, nor do I want to. There's a reason they want to stay anonymous, and quite frankly, it doesn't belong to me and isn't my business. Besides, I can't know for sure, and this is simply an educated hunch. I don't mean to sound apathetic, it's just that, I have made peace with all of this, and there's no reason that I would try to find out if others were affected. Been there, done that!! If they do exist and want to come forward, it belongs to them, and my Father. I do wish them well with their healing and am open to supporting them if they need me, but I will not try to uncover who they are. They have their journey to travel, as we all do, and for me, it's all in the past now, I must move forward.

It's difficult to explain this, but when my Father abused me, he made me feel special. He would compliment me on my body, he would say that I was funny and made me feel great overall! When the thought of other victims entered my mind, I felt used, cheap and almost felt like I was being cheated on. I felt like I had been played and that I was just another one of his toys. It was one thing to be abused while thinking that I was the only one, but this new development broke my heart and shattered my spirit!! Being in an already vulnerable stage as a teenager, I was beside myself with extreme anger and sadness. These feelings still permeate my essence to this day!!

My lack of trust of others stems from the events of that night! They are ingrained into my psyche, and even if they are well managed, for the most part, I still do experience sporadic depression and feelings of anger. I can't help it! It's like I'm hardwired to access these "go-to" emotions. Having said this, the major difference between the present and the past versions of me is that now, I don't live in those emotional states. I allow myself to feel them and then allow them to pass through me. I continuously work towards accepting who I am as a person by not resisting how I feel. I have come to understand those moments of anger, sadness, anxiety, and depression aren't permanent, they are temporary. With self-love and breathing, all suffering comes to pass!

I often wondered if I was the way I was because I was abused or destined to be this way regardless of what happened to me. That often puzzled me until one day, I realized that it doesn't matter who I am. What matters the most is, who do I want to become? So really, it's not what happens to you but, what you make of it that counts. With that being said, I am done blaming my Father for my feelings and understand that I will always be a work in progress. I also understand that there's a possibility that my Father never fully healed from his own experience of abuse, which would explain why he continued the cycle with me. Because of that, I send him Love and compassion! Even as I write this now and as you read this later.

As I write this book, one of my goals is not to have my Father portrayed as a monster. Even though he isn't present in my life, I know that some of you will see him in that light regardless of what is said or written. I don't blame you because I often have mixed feelings towards my parents. The truth is, my parents are the reason I am who I am today, the good, the bad and the ugly. Because of my toxic past, I can write this book, which will hopefully help you strive towards the best version of yourself. Take it from me; we can all benefit from developing our character! What you think of others is more a reflection of who you are as opposed to who they are. I know I have much progress in working towards dealing with my emotions. I can be a hot mess sometimes! I can lash out towards the people I love the most! I am aware of this! I am also mindful that progression isn't perfect, and I continue to progress towards bettering myself every day! I owe it to my Daughter, to my Wife and Myself!

Shortly after the events of that night, my Father was arrested because my friend went to the Police. He was the one that was in bed with me after my Father's Staff Party. Unbeknownst to me, my Father had assaulted my friends in the other room that night too. They all spoke to each other in the following days after that horrific night. My friend initially consulted another close friend who wasn't there that night about what had happened. That friend also admitted to being assaulted by my Father on two separate occasions. So that's four additional victims besides myself! Talk about a shit show! When I found out how many of my friends my Father assaulted, I wanted to kill myself!! I felt so ashamed and guilty! I thought, "If I had only gone to the Police before all this happened, they would have never been assaulted!" Even if my Father was responsible, and it wasn't my fault, I could not stop thinking that it was! Later in life, I learned that "should haves, could haves and would haves" didn't exist and even if guilt can be a bitch, continuing to live in regret would only make my life a living hell. Again, been there, done that! It is especially true when something happens that is not your fault!

My friend approached the Police because he was having nightmares about my Father coming to get him. Having experienced my own nightmares, I could relate to what he was feeling. After I stopped my Father, and he went upstairs, my friend and I had a frank conversation about the frequency of the abuse. He said something like, "Well, that was fucked up?!" and I replied, "Welcome to my world!" He couldn't believe how long it had been going on and was blown away by how often it was happening to me. To this day, I still don't remember how we managed to go back to bed. Even the next morning is blurry to me. It's like my brain blocked some of that out to protect me. It's not like we both said, "Jeez!! What a night!" "A good night sleep will fix all of this!" "See you in the morning!!" While ending it with a high-five!

Honestly, I can't imagine how my friend felt going back to sleep. Did he worry about being awakened once again? To top it off, it never dawned on me that my Father had already assaulted my friends in the other room! After my Father was arrested, my friend told me that he was worried about me and felt like, going to the Police, was the right thing to do. He did the right thing because his actions freed me, and I am truly grateful! I knew that telling the Police would cause a massive shift in my family life, and because of what happened that night, I was ready for such a shift.

CHAPTER 3

INDEPENDENCE HAS ITS COSTS!

Imagine you live in a small town, where everyone knows your name. Your Father is a well-respected Police Officer and contributing member of society. Suddenly, the news of his arrest and the assaults goes public!!! What a shock!! What a cause for public debate!

Did he do it? Do you know who accused your Father? Are you one of the accusers? Are you gay? Is your Dad gay? Were you guys gay together? What did he do to you? Did he fuck you up the ass? Did he suck your dick? Did you suck his dick or fuck him up the ass? Why didn't you tell someone? I don't believe he did it!! There's no way he did it! Your Dad's a good man and would never do that; those kids are liars! You're a liar!! Your Father's a piece of shit! You know, he almost did it to me too! How dare you make this up because your Dad didn't want to get you a car!! You're lying!!

I heard many comments, and variations of these comments come from every direction. From friends to strangers and even family members. It should come to no surprise that I developed social anxieties. Even to this day, I struggle with what people might think of me because of what happened, especially when I visit my hometown or see people from my past. It was a lot of pressure for me to handle, and to top it off; I was developing into a man at the same time. My hormones were continuously changing me physically and mentally, and puberty was hitting me with vigour. I questioned everything, my sexual orientation, the connection with family members who called me a liar, the people who wanted to help me and my friends…everything! I was suicidal before my Father was arrested, but after it all went public, and it seemed like all eyes were on me, suicide seemed like a break from the bombardment of the thoughts I had!!

Before my Father's arrest, I often joked around with friends by telling them that I would kill myself and wouldn't be at school tomorrow. They did not know that I was really contemplating suicide. They thought I was joking. If only they knew how many times I took walks in the woods near my house with the intention of ending it all. However, thinking of my Brother and Mother, I was able to summon the inner strength I needed to carry me through the ordeal, which ultimately made me stronger. I knew that killing myself would stop all the pain and negative chatter I heard at school, in town and my mind, but I was also aware enough to understand how bad it would hurt my Mother and Brother. Besides, I thought I had put them through enough already and killing myself would only make things worse. Suicide is permanent, and there would be no coming back from it. My Brother was the main reason I did not end it all. I kept thinking, "If I kill myself, who will protect him from Dad's abuse?"

My Father lost his job, and with that, most of the connections he made in our community. Some people would not believe he could do such things. Some believed the accusers, while others remained neutral. My Father was a Police Officer that did do good things within our community, and to see him in a less than favourable light was too much for some people to handle. This remains the same to this day, even after he pleaded guilty and went to prison. What I learned was that in general, people don't like seeing their heroes fall. We're seeing this more and more, now that some celebrities are being accused of acts similar to my Father's. Some don't want to believe the truth, even after many accusers/victims have come forward. Their die-hard fans do not want to think that they could do something so wrong. These die-hard fans, who worship the ground their hero walks on, even have difficulties believing that their hero is even human sometimes.

This happens because people see their heroes or people they look up to or admire as an extension of who they are as individuals. It has nothing to do with the fact that their hero has fallen but more to do with how it makes them feel about themselves, which is why it is easier not to believe the truth. I guess the same could be said about my Mother. She married my Father and had high hopes. Hoping for a bright future, filled with laughter, love and adventure, it may be too difficult for her to see him the way he really is. It may challenge how she sees herself and make her rethink some of her choices.

Also, It's one of the reasons I did not approach the Police on my own. My Father was my hero! He was charming, charismatic, well respected and loved by many of the citizens of our small community, including myself. I wanted that for myself!! I was afraid of hurting my Father and his reputation because I knew it would also hurt our reputation as a family. Even if we didn't do anything, my Mother, Brother, and I would have a permanent mark on our record.

It was almost like we were guilty by association in some way. My Mother left him after his arrest, and shortly after, we lost our house, our snowmobiles, our ATV and any other toy we had. It was all gone! It wasn't much, but when you're used to a certain lifestyle, and it's taken out from underneath you, it can be a big shock! Moving from a house with access to a forest and a river, to low-income housing where we were all crammed in these semi-detached homes was another change we needed to accept. To be honest, I didn't mind the change. I was happy not to be around my Father anymore. If losing all our stuff meant I would be free from the abuse, I was quite pleased to give all our material possessions away. It's just stuff!

We were about nine months into our new lifestyle, and my Mother decided that she would take my Father back. Because of this, she was scrutinized by some of her Brothers and Sisters for doing so. Her actions lead to a massive rift in the family. As an adult, I get where they were coming from because they were looking out for my Brother and me.

What they decided to do was give my Mother an ultimatum via letter. Remember letters? People used to write words on paper by hand and mail them to each other. Crazy right?! The letter said many things, and I vaguely remember it saying that my Grandfather would be turning in his grave because of her choices. It was signed by many of her siblings, and it hurt her deeply. You know what they say though, "You've made your bed, now lie in it!"

As blunt and unpleasant as this saying sounds, it's true! We all make decisions that have consequences attached to them; there's no denying that! Whether the outcomes are seen as bad or good will depend on the kind of decision one makes. A person that makes sound decisions generally experiences good outcomes, it's that simple! I think that my Mother had the best of intentions when taking my Father back, but I also believe that she acted out of the fear of being alone. My parents had been together for a while, and she didn't know any different. She was probably afraid of trying to find someone new. She may have seen herself as damaged goods, who knows! I remember her putting herself out there after my parents separated but I don't think it was a good experience for her. At any rate, it was brief!!

After she took him back, the family that quickly came to our aid was the same family that promptly pulled out all support. Can you blame them? I don't. They didn't want my Mother to take him back because they wanted to protect us and protect their children. They did not want to expose their children to my Father. As a parent myself, I would have made the same decision. However, when this happened, I was still in high school and thought mostly of myself, so I took this very personally. Almost like it was an attack towards me! The fact that my Father was re-establishing his way back into our lives didn't help much. I was not a big fan of having him back in my life. I was against it but like the good little boy I was, I kept my mouth shut and trusted my Mother's judgment.

Her judgment call caused a ripple effect because my Brother, Cousins, and I were tossed into this mix, forcing us to take our parents' side respectfully. The letter said something like, if she decided to take him back, we would not be welcome in their lives. It may have said that she would not be welcome or that my Father would not be welcome; it doesn't really matter. What ultimately happened was a complete cutoff from our Aunts, Uncles and Cousins alike, which sucked big time!!

Our extended family had become a big part of our lives, and having been cut off from them was a massive disappointment for me because one of my Uncles had become a Father figure to me. He was there to listen to me during many nights where we sat, just him and I, at his kitchen table. He did the very best he could to support me, given the mess we were in and the lack of experience he had, to manage it. He shared stories about his youth that he had not shared with many people, in hopes of consoling me. His support lasted for the better part of a year. When the letter was received, and the ultimatum was given, this added more confusion to my internal turmoil. It was like I was losing another Father. I was very attached to him, and the separation hurt me deeply, it left a bitter taste in my mouth. On occasion, I still feel sad when I think of all the times we missed with our Cousins, Aunts and Uncles. All this happened when I was still in my most vulnerable state, high school. I think my extended family members were hoping that my Mother would come to her senses. After all, isn't it a mother's job to protect her children from harm? They were wrong, very wrong!

People make two types of decisions in general. Decisions they can live with and others they want to forget. I have made decisions in my life that I wish I didn't make, and I'm sure you have too. The critical thing to do is learn from your mistakes, so you don't end up repeating them. Easier said than done, right?! Awareness is crucial, and I realized that one of the biggest reasons I made forgettable decisions was due to a lack of self-worth. I didn't value my life all that much, so making decisions that did not serve me became second nature. Choices like: drinking excessively, eating poorly, and negative self-talk were just a few poor decisions I would repeatedly take. Even if I wasn't suicidal anymore, I had to think more of myself; I had to strive towards something better than merely existing. Once I started building my self-worth, a funny thing happened. I drank less, ate healthier and almost eliminated all negative self-talk. I still say negative stuff to myself on occasion, but my awareness catches me in the act. It usually prompts me to say something friendly or positive about myself. It's almost like I am cancelling the negative comment I made towards myself. I think if negative self-talk can harm a person, positive self-talk must do the opposite. Right??

CHAPTER 4

MY GROUNDHOG DAY FROM HELL

Groundhog Day was a 90ies movie that starred Bill Murray, where he plays a Weatherman who is sent out-of-town for a yearly assignment where he relives Groundhog Day over and over. I chose this title because after I moved back with my family, it was like nothing happened. They lived in a new part of Canada at the time while I attended College. I had been studying to become a Police Officer, where I lived with a Cousin. It was the first time I would be on my own and the experience wasn't a success. Having my Father back in my life was still fresh and during College, he asked if he could come visit me at my apartment.

He was in town doing work for his employer and needed a place to stay for the night. I blindly accepted his request without knowing what was in store for me. I was naive to think that all would be good between us and as I transformed the couch into his bed, he insisted to sleep in my bed with me. I know what you're thinking! RED FLAG!! DON'T LET HIM SLEEP IN YOUR BED!! RED FLAG!! Looking back, how foolish was I to think that sleeping in the same bed would be a good idea! I don't know what I was thinking. We were both tired from a day of drinking and as we readied ourselves for bed, he casually asked me if we could "rub one out for old times sake." I am paraphrasing what he said but you get the idea.

Thinking that he had changed, I felt disappointed in him. It was kind of sad!! I told him no and to my surprise he asked me if I minded if he masturbate next to me. I knew that my answer wouldn't matter because he was already in that mindset. He did his business next to me and then we went to bed. I know that some of you might think that this is weird, and I would agree 100%. Looking back, I realize that I was enabling his behaviour. I could have kicked him out of my place! Heck! I could stuck to my guns, and made him sleep on the couch! I still question why I allowed this to happen. Was it because he was my Father? Was it because we had been drinking and my guard was down? Was it because I had low self-esteem and he held power over me?

One thing I know for sure is that, because I refused to participate, I experienced a win of sorts. I was saying no to the abuse and this would be the first time that I would stand my ground. Before my Father was arrested, I had attempted to say no to the abuse, on occasion. This would lead to my privileges being revoked or he would charm and guilt me until I did what he desired. Because I lived on my own, he has less power over me and this would be a defining moment for me. This would be a major turning point in my life, where I started my transition from victim to survivor. At least, that's what I thought!

Having low self esteem and addictive personality, the remaining months of College were a disaster. It wasn't a good time in my life. Having no choice but to quit college for running out of money, which I mostly drank. I felt like a dog with its tail between its legs. Forced to move back home, I was like a wounded soldier seeking refuge to heal from my experience. Little did I know, my life would be brought back to my own Groundhog Day from hell.

They say "old habits die hard," and I would come to realize that "they" were right. You would think that going to prison would be enough to change a person's ways, but this thought couldn't be further from the truth. Society is riddled with repeat offenders, and my Father was no exception. I'm taking a shower, and after rinsing the soap out of my eyes, I am surprised to see my Father watching me. I am confused, disappointed, sad and angry all in one!! Most importantly, I am caught off guard!

While looking directly at him, I say, "What are you doing here?" "You're not supposed to be in here!" My Father's reaction to my comment was pure dismissal; he didn't even bat an eye! He actually insisted that I masturbate with a hand towel wrapped around my penis because "it feels better," he said. It was like he knew I was feeling vulnerable about quitting school and instead of helping me get through it, he used the opportunity for his own selfish needs. I was so blown away by his attempt that I was in shock!! This was only a couple of months or so after his failed attempt during my stint in College. As he tried to charm me into doing what he wanted I was stunned, but managed to rinse off, wrap myself in a towel and storm out of the bathroom.

Standing in the living room, my Mother saw me leaving the washroom in disgust. While looking directly at me she said, "What's going on in there?" with an accusing tone. It was like she was blaming me! I quickly snapped back, "Why don't you ask your husband what's going on in there?" She then muttered something under her breath to the likes of "not again..." as she turned around to walk away from us. I could feel the tension in the room, and my Father didn't say much, he didn't have to. Later on, I told him that if he ever tried to pull that shit again, I would leave, and they would never see me again.

Come to think of it, why didn't I leave? Why didn't I just pack a bag full of my stuff and bounce out of there? I was about 18-19 at the time and considered an adult, so it was well within my rights. To be honest, I don't know why I didn't leave. Was it because I had just failed my first attempt at being out on my own and was afraid to try again? Was I staying because of my Mother and Brother? Did I feel like I should stay because of my Father? I really don't know. Maybe it's all of those things, and perhaps it's none of those things.

We spent the next couple of years transitioning back to our hometown. We rebuilt our family dynamic by pulling the classic "sweep it under the carpet move" many families pull when they don't want to deal with something. My Father temporarily pumped the brakes with his "attempts" towards me, and things were as normal as they could be, given our history. During this time, I returned to College, where I would meet my future Wife. What an Angel!! She had the courage of a lion and the heart of a saint; I was happy to have her by my side. She was and is the best thing that has ever happened to me in my life. Indeed the silver lining I needed to help me move passed all of it, and for that, I am grateful!! She was proof that good things happen to good people. I was a good person who deserved something positive to happen, and she was 100% that for me. I love her now as I loved her then!

We often visited my parents during weekends to hang out, help out and party. What seemed to be a smooth transition left many of our issues unspoken of as we continued to resume our family life. As we progressed, I felt this depression growing inside of me where anger became an ally, and trust seemed to be reserved only to those that didn't really deserve it at the time. A great sadness surrounded my soul, clouding my true nature. I started to mask my nature by being broken, confused and scared on the inside, while pretending all was well on the outside. I felt uneasy in my own skin, so drugs became my friends, and excessive partying became a habit. Anything to numb my feelings. My Father would occasionally attempt to rekindle his old behaviour with me, and our family life teetered between good, bad and ugly times. Some times were good, some were bad, and others got ugly...real ugly!!

One of those ugly times was when my Wife found out, through a family acquaintance, that my Father had difficulties moving on from his old ways. To be blunt, my

Father had been sexually active with a man he helped mentor, as a child, through the Big Brothers Association. I like to believe that the Universe had my back during this time because the events that lead to my Wife's random meeting with this acquaintance were nothing short of a miracle. Long story short: we were visiting friends, and my Wife went out to grab some supplies, and that's when she randomly bumped into this person. In case you're wondering, I have kept the names and places in this book anonymous for a reason. First, I have not asked for consent, and secondly, some victims haven't come forward. I want to honour them by keeping the spotlight off of them out of respect. This is why I won't be providing much detail about what happened to the victims because they have been through enough. I feel comfortable enough to tell you what I experienced because I own it, and it is part of my healing. That being said, I cannot assume that sharing the victims' stories is part of theirs.

When I found out, it thrust me back into my youth and in a depression. Waves of emotions rushed through me, and as I felt anxiety, sadness and anger, I kept thinking, "I thought he was done with all that?!" We were scheduled to visit my parents two days after finding this out, and for my sanity, I decided to pull the plug. It was my friend who suggested I cancel our visit. He said, "You know how you can get!!" "You'll wait for an opportunity, and when the moment is just right, you'll shove that in their faces!!" "You won't be able to keep that to yourself!" He was right! Verbal jousting was a forte of mine and still is to this day! I decided to cancel our visit, and I also decided to disconnect from my parents altogether. I wasn't willing to simply go along with what he did, so I called my Mother to confront her about our findings. She stated that the family acquaintance was lying. Deep down, I knew she would say that! My Mother was the one who pulled away from her siblings while putting her children at risk, remember?! My Mother would often defend my Father and his actions. She has to because it keeps the thin walls of her life together. Besides, she isn't willing to admit that my Father has "problems!!"

"How could she be lying?" I asked my mom. "She doesn't even know about dad's history!" I continued. "Why would anyone lie about something like that?" I added. Then my Mother confessed that they lied to protect me, and that made me so angry. "You lied to protect me??" I said. "You lied to protect yourselves!" I shouted. It was then that I told her that I needed space from them and that we were not going to be visiting them to which her reply was, "You're going to stop me from seeing your Daughter?" This comment angered me even more because I thought to myself, "I can't believe she is trying to blame this on me!" It's the "What's going on in there?" accusatory comment all over again!! So I said, "No, you're the one who is stopping yourself from seeing Her!" I continued to tell her that we would not be going to their place because I did not trust them anymore. All that to say, lies were told, trust was broken, and when the dust settled, I realized that I wasn't healed. Far from it, I was in dire need of self-growth and development. If I had continued in the direction I was going; I would have probably become an alcoholic or even worse, abusive towards my own family. I wasn't going to contact them until I worked out some stuff, and I wasn't even sure if I would at all. Things were fresh, and my old wounds were torn open once again!

Once we got back home and the vacation vibes wore off, I fell into a depression. I felt like I once did when I was a teenager. I felt like my Father had abused me. I was sad, depressed, anxious, confused and angry. I tried going back to work, but I could not concentrate on my job. My focus was on what happened, which forced me to take some time off work. It's exactly what happened to me when my Father was initially arrested. We were entering the exam season, and I could not concentrate. The only writing I could get on paper was my name. Luckily, the teachers were understanding and gave me passing grades. Needless to say, it wasn't the return I was looking for, but I had to rest and take time for myself. Plus, I had questions, many questions. First, I talked to my Boss and explained my situation. Her jaw nearly dropped to the ground with the news!! Despite dropping a bomb of a story on her, she was more than understanding and told me to take as much time as I needed. Telling my Boss about my life wasn't what I wanted, but I had no choice in the matter, I wasn't myself.

The second thing I did was contact the family members who still hung around my parents to tell them the news. I did this for a couple of reasons. I didn't do it to convince them not to see my parents but to remind them that leaving their kids alone with my parents might not be a good idea. I already felt guilty for not preventing my friends' assaults by remaining silent, so I wasn't about to let that happen again! From what little feedback I received through the grapevine, the consensus was that my parents did not appreciate my actions. They thought I had spoken out of turn and should have kept the information to myself. I thought, "Too bad!!" "You don't get to pretend you're operating from a higher moral position when your life is filled with lies and deceit!"

After I contacted my family members, I reached out to the man that my Father mentored and abused. I asked him how long the abuse had been going on, and I told him that I was sorry that it lead to his divorce. We had a brief conversation where he assured me that he would be OK and that I did not have to worry about him. Even if that was a tough pill to swallow, I fulfilled his request and gave him his distance. After those initial days off work, I pursued therapy and was encouraged, by my therapist, to seek growth and development. He claimed that it would benefit me and allow me to see things in a different light. He was totally right!!

We then entered the world of self-development! My intention was to become a better version of myself. I knew I was meant for more in life but was also aware enough to know that I needed to work on myself to get there. Well, work on myself, I did. For the next 3 or 4 years, my Wife and I poured it on!!! We attended seminars! We took courses and programs!!

One seminar that change my life was Unleash the Power Within. UPW is a Tony Robbins seminar, and it was awesome! It taught me how to navigate my limiting beliefs. It showed me that anything is possible if you put your mind to it. In fact, it was so good that on the first night, approximately 8000 attendees walked on fire!! That's right! We walked on fire!! I am a FIREWALKER!! Talk about a life-changing experience!! Speaking of change, we even changed our diet and overall lifestyle!! We seemed to be growing, and I felt better than I had been feeling, despite not having my parents around. Honestly, it was pretty easy to disconnect from my parents. It was like pulling an old band-aid off! We went from seeing each other often, to not at all. No text, emails or phone calls!! Completely disconnected!!

It was like the disconnection from my parents was meant to jolt us into growth and development. We now had a child, and we wanted her to grow strong physically, mentally and spiritually, so the timing of this was, for lack of better words, perfect!! This pursuit of development prompted me to write a blog about my life where I went through a chronological description of my childhood and how it affected me. This blog even prompted a reconciliation between my Mother's family and me. The Aunts, Uncles and Cousins that weren't in my life were now reading my blog and reaching out to me. Some family members who were still in contact with my parents also read my blog, and their feedback was great!

Having said this, one of my Cousins told me that she shared it with my Mother, who claimed that I was lying. I found that very interesting because my parents never read it, like at all! It's odd that the people who encouraged me the most to write a story about my life, did not approve of it, even if they did not read it. Weird eh?! I continued my growth by creating uplifting videos that I posted on YouTube and Facebook, hoping they would help others.

Things were rolling in the right direction, but somehow, I felt like something was missing.

A Healer at heart, I truly missed my parents, and I felt like mending our relationship was part of the growth I was pursuing. I held on to the idea that we could be a family, and even if I was afraid of being hurt again, I thought the gamble was worth the potential payoff. Besides, I felt emotionally and mentally stronger than before, and this seemed like the next best step for me. I thought to myself, "How could I preach growth and development while staying stagnant in the challenging areas of my own life?" It was time for me to continue breaking down the protective wall I had built inside because I knew that it was stopping the light from coming in.

So, I reached out to my parents, and we started working towards reconciliation, hoping for a better family dynamic. This and other events eventually lead to our move back to our hometown. I thought we could continue to pursue growth and development while building upon the flashes of family greatness we experienced in those early days of reconciliation. Boy, was I wrong! It's impossible to encourage someone towards growth when they think that the whole industry is a joke! I thought if I brought up insightful books I read and videos I watched during conversations with my parents that they would be interested in learning more. I soon became accustomed to their "deer in headlights look!" You know, the look someone gives you when they go somewhere else in their head. It's like they're there but somewhere else too.

After a while, I stopped sharing and even stopped pursuing growth myself. I gave it up altogether and also started regressing and repeating old patterns. I had this image of what my family should look like and wanted it for my life so desperately that I was willing to do just about anything to get it. I was willing to overlook the fact that I was now living in a town where my lifestyle didn't match the status quo. I felt uncomfortable being with my parents because our visits always seemed to revolve around drinking, and conversations were shallow and judgmental. I started drinking more on my own to cope with my social anxieties. I got more aggressive when I drank and even dragged a guy out of a local bar while tossing him out on the street because he was egging on my Father. I was becoming the man I said I wouldn't become by defending my Father. I was drowning and sinking fast!

I was also willing to overlook the fact that I wasn't creating any motivational content or reading any insightful books to better myself anymore. I was getting angrier and short-tempered with my Wife and Daughter. I even considered leaving my child alone with my parents despite my Wife's concerns. I thought, "Well, Dad only goes after boys!" You see, my Mother said this to me several times. She said it to me over the phone, when I decided to disconnect from them and a handful of times when she did not want to talk about our family issues. I genuinely think that she believes that to be true! She actually thinks that my child would be safe with them. Honestly, for a brief lapse in judgment, I thought it to be true as well. I was so focused on making our family whole again, that I was willing to believe anything. I don't think she understood why she could never have our Daughter alone.

Having put a bit of reflection on my last statement, I realize that she probably did not want to understand why she could not have my Daughter alone. It would go against the story she created in her mind about the whole situation. If she admitted that it wouldn't be wise for them to supervise my Daughter alone, the lie she held so close to her heart would unravel itself. That may be too much for her to handle.

At the time, the family image I held so close to my heart was all I could see. Putting my child in harm's way and even selling my soul was an option if it meant we could all be a functional family once again. I am forever grateful that I never left her alone with them. If my Mother was willing to ignore what had happened to my friends and me, how far would she go to ignore or cover up my Father's potential abuse towards my Daughter?? Our relationship remained superficial because any attempts at having deep conversations were met with the same rhetoric I heard many times before; "Your father has done his time!" This was my Mother's way to brush it off! It was her way to tell us not to go there! All this was tearing me apart because one of the reasons we moved back home was to repair and rebuild the relationship with my parents! It's like I said before; it's impossible to encourage someone to change when they don't see they need changing.

My marriage was now suffering and in jeopardy!! I ignored all the signs that were pointing me towards self-destruction. I was disappointed that I let it all go to shit! All the work I had done was now undone, and I felt like I could not climb out of the hole I dug for myself. I hated myself for allowing it all to happen and this created a lot of tension between my Wife and I. After a conversation about the pros and cons of staying vs. leaving, and despite our attempts at making our hometown move work, we decided to move. Ultimately, it saved our marriage. With a clearer mind and open heart, it was in our new apartment that I decided to cut ties with them completely.

Nobody wants to cut ties with their parents because it hurts like hell. I have realized that the family I wanted is dead. The family I wanted was the family I had before the abuse started happening to me, and that family doesn't exist anymore! It's nothing more than a pipe dream!! Honestly, I've made peace with that, and once I stopped chasing my lost family, things got better. A pressure was lifted from my shoulders, and I felt better! With this pressure gone, I could now focus on what mattered to me the most, my girls!! I am grateful I have my two girls with me! To me, that's all that matters!! The protective wall that needed dismantling was now more manageable, and the light continues to find new cracks and crevices to shine through. The truth is, we don't have to maintain relationships with people who are toxic in our lives, whether it be a boss, a friend, a neighbour and yes, even our parents!!

CHAPTER 5

MAYBE YOU SUCK!

What prompted me to use this chapter's title, you ask? That's simple! I wanted to illustrate that sometimes people get so caught up in their ways that they start to take themselves and their opinions way too seriously!

I haven't been around for 100 years, but I've been here long enough to know that some people tend to play the victim. These people are always complaining about how they aren't where they're supposed to be. They're never happy just being where they are because they're always looking for something better or complain about their current circumstances without any desire to change anything. They talk about having high standards, but the truth is that they are difficult and fussy. Nothing is ever good enough for them, and things never seem quite right. They complain or comment negatively about everyone they know because they think they know how everyone else should live their lives. They spend most of their time judging others to prop themselves up. They complain about not being able to connect with people when all they do is talk shit about everyone behind their backs. They don't have many connections because they are self-centred, and all they do is talk about themselves and their problems. They blame others or their circumstances and for their lack of success or happiness. They are often selfish, and if their friends aren't doing what they want to do, they will often disconnect or pout. They also have narcissistic tendencies and will often bend the truth to suit their narrative.

Who are these people? Are they your parents? Are they your neighbours? What about your children or your siblings? Well, this may come as a shock to you, but WE are these people or, at the very least, have been these people at some point in our lives. I know that I have been this person on several occasions, and even to this day, I still work towards not playing these games. It's almost inevitable, we are not perfect, we are flawed, so it seems natural to put others down because we think it will elevate us to a higher level. The truth is simple; you cannot fix yourself by breaking down someone else.

I have judged others to pump myself up. In fact, in the early years of Facebook, I was unemployed and, to be honest, quite miserable. I had a lot of time on my hands and spent most of it being a keyboard warrior, even before the term was coined. I spent hours bashing my friends' positive comments by twisting them around while trying to make them look stupid. I argued with my friends online just to prove useless points. I purposely engaged people in meaningless conversations while saying things I would never say to their faces, just to prompt a reaction. I did this because I was miserable and needed to bring people, who were happy, back down to my level, so that I could feel significant. I didn't want to be the only unhappy person surfing the web. These moments of my past taught me many valuable lessons, most notably, the lesson I want to share is: Less is best!! Saying less often means more!

I'm not sure who said this because of the conflicting sources online, but here's an excellent quote to illustrate what I mean:

"Better to remain silent and be thought a fool than to speak and remove all doubt."

Have you ever seen someone do this? Have you ever played some of these games? I have seen others purposely trigger people online just to get them going, just to piss them off!! In the biz, we call these people trolls! A troll's sole purpose is to create conflict where there was none only to fuel the fires of hatred and anger. Online trolls are great teachers in the sense that they show us how not to behave. In addition, imagine how low one must feel about themselves in order to become a troll. These people aren't happy...they can't be! They spend their time bashing and tearing down others in an attempt to make themselves feel right and feel better about themselves. They don't realize that their actions harm others and, in fact, harm themselves. I have learned that what you put out is what you get! It may not be in that exact moment, but karma has a funny way of getting you back when you least expect it. "Oh! I see you're on your way to the game?" "Here's a flat tire!" Karma is cold and swift and will strike when your guard is down and when you think all is well.

I'm no angel!! I have also blamed others or my circumstances for my lack of success. "It's my Father's fault that I am angry!" "It's because of my childhood trauma that I am not as successful as I should be!" I used to say these things in my mind all the time! I did not want to own up to my life as it was easier to blame my Father or my circumstances. I blamed the abuse I experienced for causing failed employment opportunities. I used many excuses for my failing friendships and, at the time, my failing marriage. I did this because, in a way, I wanted my Father to feel guilty for what he had done to my friends and me. I wanted my Father to feel the same level of pain I put myself through on a daily basis. That's right! The pain I put myself through!! My Father wasn't causing me pain anymore!! Playing the tapes of the memories of my past was! Keep in mind that this was before my Wife and I started pursuing our journey towards growth and development. I know that whatever I wished upon those I was blaming, I felt the full effects of those thoughts even if only internally. When I wanted someone to fail, I would fail! Whenever I wished something negative towards someone, I felt and experienced those negative thoughts and feelings! Which continued to harm me! These thoughts and evil wishes caused me much unnecessary suffering. Then, I realized that it is better to wish those around us, even if we don't like them, sincere Love and well wishes. You can't fake it until you make it with this one! It has to be real! It has to come from the heart; otherwise, it won't work!

Once I took my life into my own hands, when I took full responsibility, things started to change for the better. Instead of blaming others, I shifted the blame towards the only person that was responsible for my suffering…ME! The funny thing is, once I adopted that mindset, my suffering was alleviated tremendously. After I realized that I was responsible for the good, the bad and the ugly of my life, I started making better choices. I started reading books that would serve me. I only posted positive comments online while leaving negative ones offline. I started eating better and exercising more. All these changes brought positive experiences in my life that I never thought was possible. A good sign that you have transitioned into adulthood is when you take full responsibility for your actions and life.

Benjamin Franklin once said:
"Clean your finger before you point at my spots!"

To me, this is an excellent representation of what I mean. Look inside yourself before you cast judgment onto others. Look inside yourself and be aware of the spots and imperfections we all have. We all have flaws and weaknesses in our own lives. So before we tell someone how they should live their lives, we should make sure our lives are spotless. I mean, it's one thing to share advice with people in a mutual conversation, but preaching your unwanted opinion is inappropriate. I have had people in my adult life tell me that they wanted "what's best for me." That never sat well with me! Maybe they didn't mean to say what they did, in the way they did, but either way, my reaction has always been the same. "What's best for me?" How could this person, with their own spots and blemishes, know what was best for me? They could barely manage their own lives! That's right! I'm talking about the people in the first paragraph of this chapter. I would never say that to someone knowing what I know now. I might say, "I want **the** best for you!" and not "what's best for you." This implies that the person knows or will figure out what is best for them on their own. Everybody has an opinion about what the perfect life looks like. What's best for them may not work for someone else, and as individuals, we should mind our own business!! Unless someone is directly asking for your advice, please trust and accept that they will figure it out all by themselves.

In the great words of Bob Marley:
"Who are you to judge the life I live? I know I'm not perfect, and I don't live to be, but before you start pointing fingers...make sure your hands are clean!"

Way to go Bob! You nailed it! Taking full responsibility for our life can be challenging as it puts the onus on us and only us. Yes, it is wise to seek help to accomplish our endeavours, but ultimately, it's up to us as individuals to get shit done! Now, look into the past of your life. Look at your failures, specifically the ones where you blamed external circumstances or people. Do you have an example? If you're like me, I bet you have more than one. Having said this, can you still blame others for your failures? Have you come to the realization that it was your fault? If you can't see that your failures are your fault...maybe that's why YOU SUCK!! You're still a child!

Here is the silver lining, if we own our faults and failures, it must mean that we own our successes and victories right? Of course!! As much as you are responsible for your omissions and weaknesses, you are also responsible for your achievements and strengths. It doesn't mean that you didn't receive help on the way; it just means that you own your losses and your wins. Tony Robbins taught me this at his UPW seminar we attended. As mentioned before, I used to blame my Father for all the bad things I experienced. Until one day, I realized that if I was going to blame him for the bad, I would have to blame him for the good. Even if it's his fault for abusing me and creating the childhood drama I experienced, I would have to blame him with class and blame him for the good stuff too. I blamed him for my sense of humour which I got from watching him perform his many characters on stage and I blamed him for my knowledge of tools and how to use them. These are just a couple of positive things I got from my Father. Even if I don't have a relationship with my parents, I want to believe they tried their best, and I am at peace knowing this. Before you decide to blame anybody for your shortcomings, think about the good they have done, even if the list is short.

CHAPTER 6

BE OPEN AND FLEXIBLE

Being open and flexible are essential factors to consider when striving for growth and development. One could argue that being open and flexible are the most important factors to consider. When you open yourself to new ways of thinking or new ways of doing things, you inevitably create flow in your life. You create a life with less resistance, a life with more flexibility. A life lived in flow alleviates the need to judge others for their own choices or lifestyles as it opens you up to different opinions and lifestyles. It also makes you focus on what you're doing instead of what others are doing.

Let's say you have an unshakable opinion about a particular subject on Monday and you say to yourself, "My opinion about this will never change!" However, Tuesday comes rolling along and brings you new information about your subject, and it shakes your opinion to its core. So much so that you now contemplate and doubt your initial opinion. What do you do on Wednesday? Do you stay rigid? Do you hold on to your outdated belief because of pride? Or do you shift your opinion and become more open and flexible because of it?

Ralph Waldo Emerson said it best when he said:
"A foolish consistency is the hobgoblin of little minds!"

Today's world provides us with so much information that to remain rigid is foolish. We must seek flexibility and openness. We must allow our opinions to flip flop and adapt to new information. If we choose to remain closed and rigid, we will miss out on many opportunities for growth and development. It's that simple!! Before moving, my stance was rigid! In fact, I did not want to move. I wanted to stay in my hometown, where I was comfortable. After a conversation with my Wife, she presented me with valuable information. She talked about how great my Daughter's school would be. She spoke of the endless activities and adventures we could experience. She talked about the employment opportunities she would like to pursue in this new city and how the population was more inclined to be active. Even though I would be leaving my comfort zone, I realized that moving would bring many growth opportunities. It was this uncomfortable phase that encouraged me to write and finish this book. You never know what can happen when you open yourself up to new opinions and experiences. In fact, getting out of our comfort zone brings a lot of magic in our lives. You just have to be willing to step out of it!!

I was also very rigid about my diet. Before we started pursuing growth and development, we didn't eat very well. We thought we ate healthy, but we ate too many processed foods, too much junk food, and too much meat and dairy products. I used to joke about being a carnivore while eating the animals that ate salads and vegetables. I would make fun of Vegans and Vegetarians. After taking the Certified Coach Practitioner Course through the Healthy, Wealthy and Wise Corp., I was provided with additional online courses. With its informative and knowledge packed videos and audio clips, "Saving Lives with Fork and Knives" taught me about healthier food choices.

Since then, we tried Veganism for about 3-4 years. Later, after further consideration and research, we adopted a balanced Whole Foods Diet. You see, flip-flopping your opinions is good. Flip-flopping also taught me to be more accepting of others. I won't waste time judging people for eating what they're going to eat because, ultimately, it's their choice. At the very least, I would suggest that we all start researching what goes into our foods, by reading the labels. You'd be shocked by the ingredients in your food and what they potentially cause. The order in which the ingredients are listed on a product matters too! The higher on the list, the more of that substance is in your food. So if sugar is number one or two, that means the main ingredient is sugar! For real! So the yogurt they claim is so healthy because it's low in fat is usually packed full of sugar. Once I educated myself on the damage being caused by these ingredients, I found it very easy to shift my lifestyle. I must admit that I have not felt this good physically and mentally since my teens, and it is true what they say about abs being built in the kitchen. If I had not been open and flexible towards change, I would most likely still be eating all that junk, and my unhealthy choices would undoubtedly show up in my overall well-being.

When I think about being open and flexible, I often think about water. With its flexibility, water can get into any hole, crack or crevice without any type of resistance. I often think of myself as water, especially when approaching a difficult situation or challenging individual. I envision myself working like water, making my way towards someone's heart through the cracks and crevices one might have from building a protective wall from having a broken heart or from being hurt. Water's flexibility or softness should not be mistaken as its weakness. As soft as water can be, it can also erode even the most prominent mountain or shoreline. Take the Grand-Canyon; for example, it was the water from the Colorado River that created this colossus over time.

Like the great Bruce Lee said:
"Empty your mind, be formless, shapeless, like water. If you put water in a cup, it becomes the cup. You put water in a bottle, and it becomes the bottle. You put it in a teapot, and it becomes the teapot. Now water can flow, or it can crash. Be water, my friend".

Personally, I focus on staying flexible and open to others' opinions as best as I can to ready myself for a potential shift in the way I see things. I really focus my energy on seeing things from the other person's perspective. I find that listening to understand vs. listening to reply helps too. When we focus on understanding others, it allows us to gain clarity while being open to what is being said. When we focus on our reply, we are not hearing what the other person is saying but instead formulating our response, often missing the actual message.

I would also like to mention that physical flexibility is essential, as well. It seems to go hand in hand with being flexible and open to opinions and other ways of thinking. The importance of staying limber is often overlooked as we tend to rush through our workouts because of busy schedules and responsibilities. Even if Yoga's popularity is growing, many people still lean towards traditional activities like weightlifting, running or swimming. As good as these types of workouts are on their own, they need to have proper stretching incorporated into them. In fact, most injuries are a result of improper stretching and warm-up periods. Most of my workouts have consisted of lifting weights with some running. I am adding a Yoga practice to remain flexible as it helps avoid injuries and promotes strength. Yoga has a way of connecting the mind, body and soul. In fact, in Sanskrit, Yoga means union.

Rigor Mortis is what you get when you die, which means that being rigid is synonymous with death. The opposite goes for a flexible newborn baby! So stay flexible my friends!! Be it physical or spiritual and remain ready and open to change!

CHAPTER 7

PAIN IS INEVITABLE, SUFFERING IS OPTIONAL

What is suffering? Suffering is the result of your mental and emotional response to pain. Suffering is the meaning or emotion you attach to the pain you're experiencing.

When I talk about unnecessary suffering, I usually talk about the suffering we put ourselves through and the suffering we put others through. Both can be greatly reduced, if not eliminated if we approach the pain we experience and the pain we inflict on others with self-awareness and an open and present mind/heart. Suffering is a choice, and it is essential to realize that all pain is temporary once you accept it and move forward.

For many years, I put myself through useless suffering by replaying the clips of the abuse I experienced. I would play the clips repeatedly in an attempt to analyze the situation, hoping to find out why this happened to me. Furthermore, I would analyze why my Father would do this to me, given that he claimed to love me. I played these clips so much that after a while, they played by themselves. They became part of my inner dialogue and daily rituals, and every time my mind wandered, the clips started playing. I often experienced vivid dreams of these clips playing over and over and over. These clips became part of my habitual patterns, almost like an unintentional addiction that I could not kick! I remember getting frustrated towards myself because I couldn't stop playing the clips. This obsessive suffering caused a lack of focus and increased my anger, depression and anxiety.

Later on, I realized that the clips caused unwanted suffering and stress in my life and on my relationships with my friends and family. I had this never-ending urge to continuously control my outer environment and everyone around me because I had lost control of my internal environment. I used guilt to get people to do what I wanted and justified my actions by blaming others or my situation for my poor behaviour. This was caused because I surrendered my will power over to my thoughts while my inner storm was raging out of control. The feeling of giving control over to my thoughts lead to unwanted sadness and anger issues and often uncontrollable rage. My inner thought pattern was manifesting itself through my behaviour, which was often toxic and self-destructive. I was putting myself through a self-created inner hell, which all started with innocent day-dreaming, which eventually deteriorated into daily nightmares. This led to thoughts of suicide and alcohol and addiction-related problems. It came to no surprise that I became a problem drinker, my self-worth had almost disappeared. This is why it is imperative to love yourself because if you don't love yourself, it doesn't matter if others do, it won't make a difference.

The birth of my Daughter was one of the most critical moments of my life. I'm not sure if you'll get the reference but her birth was my own TSN turning point, if you will. This catalyst was what I needed to invoke real change. I kept thinking that I did not want to raise her where guilt and blaming was part of her upbringing. I did not want her to feel like she needed to manipulate others to be loved, and I didn't want her to feel like she was being manipulated into love. I also wanted her to be proud of me because she would eventually be old enough to understand my story, and I wanted her to think, "Yeah, he's been through a lot, but he's still kicking ass!" I also knew that there was more to my life and that I had a higher calling waiting for me. I also realized that I was worthy of it and that I deserved to experience it fully with all its joy and bliss.

This led to a shift in my thoughts, at the very least, a shift in the perception of my thoughts. I now understood that the clips (I), not what my Father did, were creating all this suffering. Also, I realized that I could change my situation. Yes, my Father was the initial cause of my pain, and I am not minimizing that. Having said this, it was the fact that I played the clips ten thousand times (or probably more) that created all my additional suffering.

Have you ever experienced something like this? I'm sure you have. It doesn't have to be an example related to abuse; it can merely be something someone said to you. For example, picture yourself in a conversation with your best friend, and he or she says something that leaves you feeling sad. Instead of dealing with it instantly by talking to your friend, you push it down by saying nothing. As you go about your day, you keep hearing what that person said in a loop, and that initial feeling of sadness keeps growing and growing. You keep thinking to yourself, "I should of said this!" or "I can't believe my friend would say that to me!" You churn and churn the conversation over in your head until your initial feeling of sadness morphs into anger and irritability. This spills over into your job and the people you interact with over the course of your day. You are now irritable and angry towards everything and everyone because of what your friend said. As you get home, you are greeted by your dog/spouse/child and instead of being happy to see them, you are tired, worn out and not in the mood for pleasantries. Your day hasn't gone the way you wanted it to, because you were affected by what your friend said. You allowed an external event capture your inner peace while holding it hostage all day!! That's what suffering is!! What that person said may have cut you initially, but it was your constant poking at the wound that pushed you over your emotional edge.

My Father once told my Brother and I that we were stupid. I forget exactly why but it had something to do with a chore we did wrong. I do remember where I was and even remember the sun shining through our patio door. For years, I hated being called stupid! I hated it with a passion! I suffered through a thousand or more clips of my Father saying those words over and over until it became part of my

DNA. When people called me stupid, I did not see them. I saw my Father calling me stupid all over again!

Lady Bird Johnson said this:
"Children are likely to live up to what you believe of them."

This suffering even provoked a couple of violent confrontations with two good friends of mine. It also led to an altercation between my Father and me after my Cousin's wedding all because he said: "Your wife can be so stupid sometimes." We were all gathered at my Aunt and Uncle's house for my Cousin's wedding. It was a beautiful wedding, an outdoor wedding. My Aunt and Uncle lived on this majestic waterfront property that gently sloped towards a River.

Many people were attending my Cousin's special day. Aunts, Uncles, Cousins and people I knew from high school gathered as my Cousin tied the knot. One of the guests was a man that my Father, as a Police Officer, had arrested several times when he was younger. This man took it upon himself to seek revenge that night. He was very aggressive towards my Father by bumping into him and even spilled his drink all over my Father on several occasions. Needless to say that this man was putting a damper on our night, and I was getting irritated. To add fuel to the situation at hand, it was an open bar! Because I drank excessively at the time, I took full advantage of the free beer! My Father wasn't doing much to respond to the man's behaviour because he was present enough to understand where he was and how he should carry himself in that situation. It wasn't the time to try and pick a fight! We were at a wedding!! Besides, I couldn't believe that the man, who was also the Groom's Best Man, would act so poorly! I was blown away by his lack of restraint and common sense!

So imagine this!! You're at a party, and everybody's having a great time. Everybody's having drinks, and the party is happening. You're enjoying yourself and feeling great, but suddenly, someone you barely knew, comes out of the shadows just to mess with you and the people in your group. How would you react? What would you do? Here's what I regrettably did; I pushed him to the ground. I had had enough of this man!! How dare he hold my good time like it was some sort of hostage in a bank robbery. Plus, I was subconsciously dealing with my own demons and used the situation as a means to unleash the beast within me. It was like I was permitting myself to sink to his level, and in that brief moment, it felt good. I'm not super proud of what I did, but given the circumstances and context of the situation at the time, I felt like my actions were justified.

So after the man got up, it is needless to say that he wanted to fight me. At that moment, I was open to the challenge. I remember thinking, "this isn't going to last long, either I kick his ass, or he kicks mine." Luckily, we were separated even before anything happened, and shortly after, we decided to leave. It wasn't that late when we got to my parents' place, so we continued partying. My parents had a hot tub, and the girls and my Brother went in it to chill out. My Father and I were sitting down, having a beer while talking about the man at the wedding. We were getting primed up and even considered going back to the wedding to settle the unfinished business. As we recounted the night's events and contemplated our silly plan, my Father said, "Your wife can be so stupid sometimes!" He was referring to when she stepped in to separate the potential fight. She did this a couple of times that night, and I am thankful she did. Her actions helped alleviate the tension between us men by buying us time to think instead of reacting. I asked him to stop saying she was stupid, as I did not like that. Who would?? Instead of listening to my simple request, he doubled down to call her stupid an additional two times.

At that moment, I felt like he was calling me stupid all over again! Just like when I was a kid! Given that we were already agitated, it didn't take much for us to use the pent up energy we had against each other. I remember getting so mad and furious that I shouted, "Stop calling her stupid!" while smashing the beer bottle I was holding on the side table next to me. He took his bottle and did the same, breaking it on the coffee table in front of him. Glass and beer flew everywhere, and at that moment, a flash of clarity hit me as I thought, "Are we about to kill each other?" I dropped the bottle and rushed outside for some fresh air. I was still furious! I stepped outside, and I made my way towards the camper next to the house, punching out both its windows. As I pulled my arm out from the second punch, and the blood was pissing out everywhere, I said aloud, "I immediately regret that decision!" In a panic, I rushed inside blood gushing everywhere, my Mother handed me a towel to stop the bleeding. The others rushed into the house to see what all the commotion was. Both my Wife and Mother were in shock but hurried to get dressed to bring me to the hospital. Over 150 stitches and 5 hours later, my Mother drove my Wife and I back to their place where my Dad and I quickly patched things up, as we often did, so that my Wife and I could leave to go back to our house. To this day, I still feel the consequences of that night, and as I write this sentence, I still have glass in my arm.

Pretty intense, right? I know! As I edit this, I can't believe I was so careless! I could have seriously injured myself, and my life would have turned out much differently. Sadly, this would not be the only time my Father and I would be at each other's throats! Every time it happened, we would do the same thing, sweep it under the carpet! A quick hug or a handshake, and all was forgotten. Not dealt with, but forgotten!!

Even if my Father could have chosen better words, it was the clip that I replayed over and over in my mind that triggered an emotional response to the pain I felt when I was called stupid as a child. It was all that suffering that eventually led to all that unnecessary violence.

I knew that I that I would benefit from reducing the suffering and the pain in my life and in the lives of others. Remember this, when you suffer needlessly, not only does it impact your life, but it also affects the lives of others. My thoughts had me stuck in the victim state, and I was so angry. Angry towards myself for letting my Father do those things to me and some of my friends and mad that I kept replaying the clips repeatedly. I was overwhelmed with anger, so it comes to no surprise that I would lose my lid over trivial things like having to wait for a red light.

Furthermore, I was so prone to using anger as my "go-to" emotion that my brain got addicted to being angry. I actually liked the feeling I got when angered. I would overreact over small things because I felt powerful in "Angry Mode." I felt like the Incredible Hulk, minus all the superpowers, all I had was the anger. Little did I know, I was burning myself out by engaging my Fight or Flight response on a daily basis. Even though my behaviour often challenged my marriage, I am grateful that my Wife accepted me for who I was and not who I was acting like.

I knew that relieving the suffering in my life would, in fact, make the world a better place. I knew this because it would help reduce the amount of suffering in the lives of others around me, which would hopefully start a chain reaction.

Antoine de Saint-Exupéry said:
"One's suffering disappears when one lets oneself go, when one yields - even to sadness."

The first thing I did while pursuing self-healing was to forgive myself for creating all this unwanted suffering. I cut myself some slack and realized that I was caught in a brief moment that had gone unchecked for too long. I knew that forgiving myself would be crucial to my continuous improvement. Without forgiveness, I would be lost in a perpetual cycle of self-created suffering. Plus, how could I forgive others if I could not forgive myself? Then, I started looking inside myself for all the areas of my life where there was unwanted suffering. Once I did this, and this was very important, I became self-aware of the many facets of suffering I had created, and it was like I experienced an awakening.

Self-Awareness was key to my initial call to action as it put the onus on me instead of looking outwards for a solution. It challenged me to realize that I was to blame for all my suffering and not some external force. Being self-aware also provide me with a sense of release because I could take charge of my life instead of blaming others for why I was feeling the way I was. I also realized that if I was to blame for all my failures, I could also blame myself for all my victories. I started catching myself playing the clips of suffering, and instead of getting angry and frustrated towards myself, I would immediately forgive myself and play a clip of happiness. I would play clips of my Daughter smiling or my Wife giving me a bear hug, anything to interrupt my old thought pattern. I want to suggest that you do the same. Next time you're replaying thoughts in your mind that don't serve you, catch yourself doing it! Then, I challenge you to interrupt your thought pattern by changing your thinking to something that will benefit you.

I started crowding out my internal suffering by replacing it with inner joy and feelings of happiness. Even if those initial days were challenging, they provided me with a renewed sense of peace, which made me smile for no reason. I had not smiled for the sake of smiling for a long time. Crowding out my suffering with happy memories helped me reduce the amount of anger I experienced daily, which meant, no more frustrated tantrums at red lights.

Now that I was working on my inner growth, I continued to explore areas where I was causing internal and external suffering. I knew that I would be developing myself for the rest of my life, which excited me! What fascinated me then and still now was when I opened the gates of my Essence/ Soul/Spirit, I started getting signs of additional areas in my life that needed development. Call it God, the Universe or even the Force if you're a Star Wars fan, but life tends to send people the lessons they need to learn when they need to learn them. The problem is, for many of us, we are too egocentric to notice these "Ah! Ha!" moments. We go through life, blaming and judging others when we should be looking at ourselves, and this egocentric behaviour causes an unfortunate cycle of repeating the same mistakes over and over and over until you die. It's sad but true! My questions for you are: are you aware enough to notice these "Ah! Ha!" moments in your life? If so, will you answer their call?

So, as you can see, suffering is something we create ourselves, and just because we go through our lives experiencing pain, it doesn't mean that we have to suffer through the experience. Remember that pain is inevitable; suffering is optional.

CHAPTER 8

LET'S GET PHYSICAL THROUGH BODY LANGUAGE

Our body language dictates and projects our level of confidence and overall well being. In general, you can tell a lot about someone's personal life by the way they carry themselves physically. What I have learned about body language is that, if you change it, it changes you. What I mean by that is, if you are feeling down or depressed, the odds are you have also adopted body language or a posture that matches your inner state of mind. That means that the first thing you should do to change your state of mind is change your physiology. If you change your physiology, your mind will follow.

I'm not saying that all you have to do is change your posture to have a happy life. That would be lazy on my behalf to suggest. What I am suggesting is that when you change your posture first, it will be easier for the mind to follow. Even the Children's Superstar Raffi had a song called "Shake your sillies out!" where it asks children to shake,

shake, shake their sillies out! When my Daughter was 5-6, we played this song on numerous occasions at home to foster a lighter and more loving environment. If you swap out the word sillies for any other word that describes a low state of mind, the principle would still apply. First, you must start by shaking whatever sillies you have out of your system before the mind will be open to doing the same. Even Eckhart Tolle suggests that, after two ducks get into a fight, each duck flaps its wings vigorously several times. They do this to release any surplus energy that built up from the confrontation. Once the excess energy is released, the ducks go about their business peacefully and forget it even happened. Ducks don't hold on to grudges as it would appear that they shake their sillies out too!

I have noticed that I am happiest when I carry myself in my best posture. It keeps me light on my feet. I imagine a rope pulling my chest forward, which causes my shoulders to pull back and my head to pull up naturally. Go ahead and try it! In today's world, we often have our hands stretched out in front of us either while working from a desk or at home on our computers or while driving! Doing these types of activities over a long time, creates strain in the body.

Our addiction to Smartphones has affected our posture as well. We put a lot of strain on our neck when we look down towards the screen. By correcting your posture, you are opening your diaphragm. This allows your lungs to dilate, taking in more air fully, and in return, makes you sharper. When I help people with self-esteem issues, the first thing we look at is their resting posture. People who keep their heads in a lower position with their shoulders pulled forward tend to have confidence issues because of their restricted diaphragm. It's as if they don't want to be seen or noticed and have adopted a posture that doesn't promote confidence. It comes from their subconscious mind, and it's like they feel they are not worthy of oxygen, hence the compressed diaphragm. I used to have a weird breathing pattern in College. I would breathe in, pause for second or two, release the air, pause again, and inhale. I did this subconsciously and didn't even notice I was doing it. It was the student sitting next to me who noticed how I was breathing and pointed it out. She said, "you breathe weird!" I had never realized it, but I saw how my breathing had no flow and no natural rhythm. It was choppy, shallow and unnatural. I now understood why I was struggling with my studies. My brain was lacking oxygen! I don't know when I started that breathing pattern or why I started it. Maybe it was a result of the abuse I survived; maybe it manifested itself before, who knows! A restricted diaphragm will hinder your air intake, making you sluggish and less sharp, feeling almost asleep. It's important to breathe deeply, and I don't know if you know this but, oxygen is free, and you can have as much as you want!!! Aren't you glad I shared that information with you? I don't pass that around to just anybody!

I know this might sound too simple of a concept, but I encourage you to take three deep breaths before any significant decision. Filling your bloodstream with oxygen helps clear your mind and helps put you in a state of calm. Try it now!! Make sure you're sitting down because if you're not used to deep breathing, you might experience dizziness.

DO NOT ATTEMPT WHILE DRIVING!! In fact, if you experience some dizziness, it should be a sign that you don't breathe deep enough. Train yourself to breathe deeply, and it could transform your life. I have had people tell me that once they changed their physiology and breathing, people approached them in a different way. They felt more respected and even more attractive. I believe that once you command yourself into adopting a higher standard, explicitly concerning your body language, people usually match your standards. It's like you attract like-minded people. Again, your body language will dictate and project your confidence level and how people will see you.

Also, your confidence level dramatically affects your interactions with people. We even use our body language to build rapport with everyone we meet. Building rapport is essential for creating and maintaining relationships.

As Tony Robbins would say:
"Rapport is Power!" "Rapport is created by a feeling of commonality."

The more you have in common with someone, the more likely you are to like, befriend and trust that person. A common mistake most people do is wait until they have spoken enough words with someone before deciding if they will like that person. The issue with that is, based on the consensus of my research, the verbal part of communication accounts for about 7%. That means people leave out about 93% of their potential communication skills. Great rapport is when you meet someone and you both connected over a short period of time, you simply clicked.

There's a reason this happens, and maybe it has happened to you! You're at a party, and you meet someone for the first time. Within a short time frame, you felt like you were both on the same page or thought this person had good vibes. You might have called it a spark or that you both clicked. The reason you both clicked was that you naturally connected both on the physical and verbal level. I'm not necessarily talking about a sexual connection here, although that happens as well. When I met clients for the first time, my primary objective was to build rapport with them as soon as possible to create a bond. Once the relationship was created, I could focus on the underlining issues that were causing them their suffering. This was made possible because they trusted me or, at the very least, felt like they could trust me.

So, I guess the question is, "How do I build rapport?" To build rapport, you must consider this. It is a simple skill to work on as we all do it naturally, albeit some do it better than others. Once developed, you will feel more connected to people as you will know how to build rapport with them quickly. In return, this will help you build your confidence. I think self-awareness plays a big part because once you are aware of your natural skills, you can further develop them. Even Spiderman needed to practice his newly acquired skills before becoming a Superhero.

As mentioned before, the breakdown of communication goes like this: 7% verbal, 93% non-verbal. The verbal aspect of communication is essentially the words that we use to speak to each other. The non-verbal aspect of communication has its own breakdown. The non-verbal accounts for 55% body language and 38% tone of voice. To elaborate a little further on the non-verbal, it accounts for things like style, expression, tone, facial expression, the tempo of voice and posture, to name a few. This doesn't mean that the words we use aren't necessary. In fact, I will talk about Neuro-Linguistic Programming in the next chapter.

Most of us know how to speak, but not many of us really know how to communicate effectively. Again, most people wait until they have so many words between them before rapport is developed. What we often overlook is how we can build rapport by using our non-verbal. It's called Mirroring and Matching, and I think it was first pointed out by the late Dr. Milton Erickson. He would study people and noticed that those who seemed to be connecting would often be mirroring and matching each others' movements to some degree. They may be leaning the same way, tapping their feet the same way and often speaking with the same tone of voice. You can probably guess what the people who didn't connect looked like. One person checking their phone while the other looks at the ceiling. Need I say more?

Speaking of cell phones, please put them down when having a conversation!! Take the time to look them in the eyes once and a while; it won't kill you! Specifically, if you're on a date and talking face to face!! Imagine the vibe you're sending out when you pay more attention to your device than the person you're talking with. You are literally saying that the phone is more important than the conversation you're having with that person. I had a client complain about the fact that he wasn't getting any interviews. When I asked him about how he presented himself to potential employers, he told me that he would hand out resumes while wearing his earbuds.

To top it off, he said that he didn't initiate much conversation while handing out resumes because his music was on. He was confused as to why he wasn't getting any interviews. Really?!?!?! I had to explain to him why it was important to leave his phone and earbuds in his pocket. Would you interview someone that seemed like they didn't care enough to "unplug" for a second? I wouldn't!! You must understand that it's all communication, whether you're speaking or not. The employer probably thought, "really, you can't even take your earbuds out for a second??" "I'm not giving this guy an interview, how is he going to handle my customers??" This is why it is imperative to build rapport if you want to make a great first impression, especially when searching for employment.

What I do to build rapport with people is mirror how they sit and speak, and before long, I have entrained them into matching me. What I mean is, when I follow their movements for a while, I can implement a change, and after I do this, a high percentage of people will match what I do. This is a clear indicator that we have started to create and build rapport. It also shows me that they are engaging in the conversation by their level of attention.

Example: a client is leaning towards me in his/her chair without crossing their legs while I mirror them for about 5-10 minutes. We chat about light stuff, like the

weather and how the client's job search has gone so far. Then, I implement a change to the way I sit; let's say I cross my legs and sit back in my chair. After I have done this, the client usually adjusts the way they're sitting to match my style. Once that happens, I know that we've started building rapport and as long as I continue to mirror and match them, I know that they are likely to be open to my suggestions and possibly open into going deeper where we talk about their life's struggles.

Why is building rapport important? Well, it is important to develop rapport building skills in life because it is the foundation of our communication. Before we used language and words to communicate with each other, we mostly let our bodies do the talking. We used symbols, hand gestures, grunts, drawings, dancing, and even acting to express ourselves. After verbal language was developed, the need for grunting and hand gestures diminished. Except for French people!! Just kidding!! As the years turned into decades and then centuries, our language evolved, and the art of building rapport through body language wasn't as prevalent. That is why using your physicality to build rapport is so important! It's in our DNA!! Mastering the art of using body language to communicate will provide you with an additional tool.

Whether we use it for business or personal, it is how we fully connect with people while developing meaningful friendships, relationships and partnerships. Don't forget, we all do it naturally, and if you can tune into your natural abilities, the odds of developing them increases tremendously. Take the time to practice this with people, you know, without telling them what you're doing!! If you can successfully entrain people you already have rapport with into following your patterns, you should be able to do it with people you don't know. At least, that has been my experience.

CHAPTER 9

NEURO-LINGUISTIC PROGRAMMING

What is Neuro-Linguistics Programming? Based on the Linguistic Society of America, *"Neurolinguistics is the study of how language is represented in the brain: that is, how and where our brains store our knowledge of the language (or languages) that we speak, understand, read, and write, what happens in our brains as we acquire that knowledge, and what happens as we use it in our everyday lives." (https://www.linguisticsociety.org/resource/neurolinguistics)*

In addition, NLP is a tool that can help create permanent change and eliminate any negative states, habits or beliefs that are holding a person back. The part I want to focus on specifically is the "what happens as we use it in our everyday lives." I first learned about neuro-linguistics as I was completing my Certified Coach Practitioner training through the Healthy, Wealthy and Wise Corporation. We talked about toxic and non-toxic words and the importance of using non-toxic words. I'd like to go even further by saying that you can also have toxic thoughts and non-toxic thoughts. Just because you aren't saying it doesn't mean that you're not thinking it. The brain doesn't know the difference between what is real and what is imagined.

Henry Ford put it best when he said:
"*Whether you think you can, or you think you can't – you're right!*"

He means that if you often say, "I can't do this or can't accomplish that," your brain will take your statements at face value and manifest your thoughts until they become your reality. The same goes if you're saying, "I can do this, or I can do that." Your thoughts will literally become your reality.

Of course, you won't become a Rock Star, as you sit and wait on your couch by merely saying "I am a Rock Star, I am a Rock Star, I am a Rock Star!" Even the "Little Engine That Could" knew that saying "I think I can, I think I can, I think I can!" while putting her best effort forward would eventually yield the results she was after. Even if this book was used to teach children about the value of optimism and hard work, it truly transcends into adulthood and applies to the pursuit of one's goals/dreams. I believe that people must first believe in themselves before they'll achieve any goal they set their minds to. It's that simple! Figure out what your goal is, believe that you can achieve it by saying it to yourself and then put your best effort towards what you want to achieve and sooner or later, you will get there.

You must get real, though!!! I have always wanted to write a book about how I turned my life around for the better but never put any effort forward, until now. Even now, as I write this book, I always tell myself, "I am writing a book, I am writing a book!" I also go as far as believing that the book is already written, and all I have to do is put it down on paper. Because I have changed my thoughts and the way I speak to myself, I am now convinced that I am merely a positive belief and step away from achieving any goal I set my mind to.

To quote Dr. Wayne Dyer:
"Change your thoughts, change your life!"

When I started developing my self-awareness, I realized that I was using many toxic words towards myself. These words often sabotaged my success by unconsciously leading me towards failure, disappointment and frustration. I also noticed that toxic words affected my confidence and attitude. I would often say, "I'll try my best!" when attempting anything, which led to many incomplete projects, goals and dreams. I realized that using the word "try," I was actually giving my future self an excuse for why I didn't achieve or complete my task. It was almost like I knew I wouldn't do it, so I would say, "I'll try!" This attitude of "trying" without achieving results affected my self-esteem. I would get fired up about doing something new but would follow the path of least resistance in my mind, which triggered the "I'll try!" statement or thought.

Some other toxic words I have used and still catch myself using from time to time are: should have, could have, would have, can't, someday, if, maybe and but. Did you know that using "but" negates everything you said before the "but"?

Pierre Lafontaine

Here's an example, "You are a nice person but can come across as being rude." Again, what you really want to say is, "You come across as being rude!" or even "You're rude!" Instead, we sugar coat our thoughts in order to protect ourselves from being judged and not loved. We may also do it in an attempt at protecting the person we are talking to.

This goes without saying that non-toxic words can motivate, persuade and influence people to believing change is easy. Some of these non-toxic words are: easily, naturally, aware, experiencing, realize, unlimited, expanding, before, after, because, now, abundant, possibility, create and visualize. Knowing and applying these words will **naturally** and **easily** support any change you strive towards. See what I did there?!

It goes even further than that. Using toxic words towards yourself can affect your physical health and lead to unwanted anxiety and depression. If you continuously say to yourself, "I'm stupid!" It will become part of your inner dialogue, and eventually, your subconscious mind will start believing it!

This kind of thought pattern will lead you down a road of constant failures; there's no other way around it! You will have programmed yourself to think that way! Thinking like that can create a perpetual cycle of victimization, and you might start to feel like life is happening to you instead of for you. Most of us have this person in our inner circle that often plays the role of the victim, and if you don't know who it is, it's probably you!! All kidding aside, this person always seems to be experiencing drama/hardship and is often complaining about their lives and how bad it is. They frequently talk about changing by using the good old word "should." "Yeah, I should do this and should do that." These people are very hard on themselves because toxic words are a significant part of their vocabulary as they use them all the time.

In addition, whether they want to admit it or not, they like it when the conversation is focused on them and their problems because it makes them feel significant and is often their source of love. The interesting thing is that this type of person usually doesn't know they are the drama queen of the group because it is part of their habitual patterns. They will often get defensive when confronted about it. I like encouraging self-awareness with people like that by asking them to use better words to describe themselves. So, if someone makes a mistake and says, "I can be so dumb!" I quickly say, "I don't think you're dumb, we all make mistakes, and you're a human being, bound to make your own."

Our brains are like organic computers and are programmed from birth. As we grow older, the software in our minds continues to update itself. The issue is, our software is updated based on the perception we have about our circumstances, the things we hear and see and the people that surround us. So, if you are surrounded by toxic conditions and toxic people using toxic language, your software will use that information to update itself. In return, this could affect the level of toxicity you experience in your own life.

I don't own the following quote but have used it often, and I'm sure you've heard it at least once in your life. ***"If you hang out with assholes long enough, you'll become one!"***

As much as this quote can be crass, it can also be very accurate. This phenomenon happens at the subconscious level because we want to be liked by our peers. We want to be accepted and loved by them, which is why we tend to become who we hang out with the most. It's just the way it goes!

What's impressive with all of this is that you can program your brain into using non-toxic words as well, all it takes is little self-awareness. When I started my growth and development journey, I noticed that I would often say or think to myself "You're so stupid!" as a result of not getting a concept right away, or not being able to do something the first time. It was my awareness that allowed me to challenge this pattern. I started asking, "Is that true, am I stupid?" I knew the answer was a hard no therefor; I would correct myself when saying or thinking that I was stupid. Being aware of my toxic thoughts reduced the frequency of negative thoughts entering my mind. It took some time but, if I can do it, so can you. You have to be patient with yourself, focus on progression as it will take time and effort, but eventually, you'll be using better words towards yourself and others.

I would also like to mention that your everyday language makes a big difference towards how you feel about yourself and others. What do you say when someone asks you, "how's it going or how are you?" I have heard many variations, but the common responses are "fine", "good", or the ever-popular, "not bad". Fine??? Good??? Not bad??? I mean, come on!! We can do better than "fine, good or not bad?" Let's face it; life is wonderful, fantastic and outstanding. The gift of waking up every morning isn't a given; nothing is guaranteed. I continuously make a conscious effort to realize that nothing is a given but is actually a gift. With that being said, I choose better words to describe my feelings, thoughts, and things around me so that I can lead a positive and loving life.

Remember this, the longest conversation you'll ever have is with yourself, so be kind, cut yourself some slack and choose better words to describe yourself and the world around you!

CHAPTER 10

CONDITIONING

From birth, our parents and our environment shape and influence our development. Every aspect of our life is greatly influenced by our parents' decision towards how they raise us. If your Mom loves Celine Dion, there's a good chance you'll enjoy that type of music or a genre similar to it. If your Dad is a Toronto Maple Leafs fan, you'll probably end up liking Golf!! Just kidding!! You know what I mean. My Father was a Montreal Canadiens fan, and the only hockey team we watched at home was the Habs. Even if the NHL has 31 teams and I have been living on my own for almost 20 years, I am still a Habs fan!! It's ingrained into my identity! I don't see myself following any other team! This phenomenon is called conditioning.

Having said this, the conditioning you receive as a child is as good as the person doing the conditioning. I realize now more than ever that I was conditioned into thinking that what my Father was doing to me was OK. I was groomed into believing that the relationship I had with my Father was a healthy and normal one. Now, as an adult, with several therapy sessions under my belt, I know that it was very toxic and damaging.

Jim Morrison said this about conditioning:

"The most loving parents and relatives commit murder with smiles on their faces. They force us to destroy the person we really are: a subtle kind of murder."

To explain conditioning a little further with my own experience, I would have to say that I kind of got used to being abused. At first, it was weird, and I wasn't sure what to make of the experience, but because of how often it happened to me, it became easier to handle. Eventually, it actually became part of my identity and everyday life. It happened so often that after a while, I kind of liked it. I was so used to being abused that I didn't mind when it happened, I actually expected it. A story that comes to mind is when my parents owned and operated a fishing lodge. It was the end of the season, and My Father and I were in the process of closing down the facility. One night, I was drinking with some girls, and when I went to bed, all I wanted to do was sleep. My Father kept pulling and tugging at me to try to get me to masturbate with him, but I refused. Out of anger, he ejaculated on my back in a "That's what you get for disobeying kind of attitude."

Sadly, I was so used to this kind of treatment that it didn't bother me; in fact, nothing happened the next morning. We did not talk about it, and it was business as usual. It took me a long time to realize that even if I did enjoy the attention my Father was giving me, I wasn't really enjoying the sexual abuse. I truly enjoyed the love and attention he seemed to be showing me because I was used to it. Those awkward moments were extremely toxic and would end up being the primary source of my pain and suffering as an adult.

As you can imagine, this was very confusing for me. For years, I questioned my sexuality. I even thought I was gay. I kept thinking, "How can I not be gay? I keep doing this gay shit with Dad, and I'm enjoying it, so I must be gay!" I was eager to please my Father because I adored him. I trusted him 100% with what he was doing. When you trust a person who holds a position of power over you, specifically your parents, you trust them to take care of you and make the right decisions to help you, not to harm you. Unfortunately, it doesn't always work out that way. Having said this, I think that people in general, are always trying to make the best decisions they can in any given moment based on their own conditioning and upbringing. I don't think my Father had the intention of harming me; it just happened that way. He may have never really come to terms with what his Father did to him as a child, which is why he didn't understand the severity of his actions. I had a conversation with him once, and he said that if my friends had been 18 years old, he would have never been arrested, and it would have never been blown out of proportion. He continued to defend his actions by claiming that my friends liked what he did to them. I remember saying quite bluntly that they didn't, then he gave me the "let's agree to disagree" face. He was so conditioned into believing the same lies I believed in that I'm not sure he fully understood the implications of his actions. One of the significant things that separates me from him is that he was caught and imprisoned while my Grandfather wasn't. That's what broke the cycle. I knew the abuse was wrong and when my Father was arrested, his fairy-tale ended and reality came crashing on him like thunder before a storm. After the abuse was out in the open and other adults supported my initial thoughts towards the abuse, I knew I would never do to my children what he did to me.

While working in the Employment and Social Services sectors, I have heard many clients claim that they were born depressed or anxious. Some even claimed that they inherited their mental illnesses because of their genetics. Even if there might be some truth to their claims, I'm not fully convinced that their genetics are solely responsible for their suffering. In addition to their claims, I think what also happens is that they inherited their parents' lifestyle. Similar to the Celine Dion example, we are prone to be like our parents. The baseline of our personality comes from adopting parts of our parents' traits. As we grow up and develop, our personalities evolve towards adapting to external factors such as our friends and experiences outside life at home.

Think about it! During your early years on this planet, you spend a lot of time with your parents and will naturally observe them as they interact with you, with each other and with their friends. It should come to no surprise that you would model their behaviour and attempt to copy their traits to a certain extent. As humans, we want to feel loved and belong, so fitting in is something we naturally pursue.

When somebody claims that they were born depressed or anxious solely because of genetics, I often ask about their parents' lifestyle. The client will usually state that their parents showed signs of depression and anxiety all their lives growing up. Again, I think it's the combination of genetics and parents' lifestyle that helped shape their personality and mental illness. The client had no other choice but to learn the same type of behaviour, in some shape, way or form. Their parents, who learned behaviour patterns from their parents, passed on the same habitual patterns they learned onto their children. The only way this varies is if a change in the cycle is made. Having said this, it is almost impossible to make a change if you're unaware of your patterns.

My Father was abusive towards me because his Father was abusive towards him, and if we dig deep enough, we would probably discover that someone, in a position of power, was probably abusive towards my Grandfather. Back then, things like that stayed within the family and were kept on the down-low, never to see the light of day. In fact, keeping family secrets under wraps was common back then, and most families of the era had a skeleton or two in their closet. Even with today's technology and social media platforms, some families still keep dark secrets to themselves. We fear being judged so much that we would rather live a toxic home life than seek the help we would most likely benefit from. All that because we worry what others might think of us.

As I mentioned before, the cycle was broken when my Father was arrested. It was a bittersweet moment for me, being the primary victim and all. I knew what my Father's arrest would mean for us as a family because, at the time, I had seen a news special that reported a very similar situation to ours. A man who sexually abused his boys was arrested and eventually convicted, and because of his arrest and loss of employment, they lost everything. I knew our family would meet a similar fate because my Father would most likely lose his job.

This was one of the reasons I kept quiet for so long. I knew that everyone in our town would know, including friends and family. I feared losing my friends due to being judged, and quite frankly, I was ashamed. It's bad enough to have been abused, but being sexually abused added a whole other dynamic. I was already confused about my sexuality, and I feared people might think that I was gay. I should add that I believe there is nothing wrong with being gay. I don't care who you love and choose to spend your life with! Period!! Remember this happened in the 90ies and the last thing a straight teenage male wants is to be perceived as being gay. I loved my Father, but I knew what he was doing to me was wrong, and when the story broke loose in our small town, I felt a great sense of relief because I knew I was saved.

I am so grateful that I realized that if you can be conditioned into believing a bad lifestyle is good for you, you can also condition yourself into adopting a lifestyle that will promote health, growth and development. A great example of this was when my Wife and I started exploring our intimate sides. There were places that she could not touch me as they left me feeling as I felt when I was intimate with my

Father. She couldn't touch me in certain places as it triggered flashbacks of abuse, causing me unwanted anxiety. It felt like I was brought back into those situations in real time.

For context purposes, I think it's important to distinguish the difference between having sex and making love. Before meeting my Wife, I had had sex before without experiencing any flashbacks. Having said this, most of my one night stands involved alcohol. Having sex is great, but making love is divine. As weird as this may sound, when I was intimate with my Father, it was like we were making love. I was too young to understand how toxic and wrong it all was. To add fuel to the fire, I loved my Father, and he loved me. It wasn't like we had a one night stand as the abuse was a daily thing for many years. So when I hooked up with women, it was merely a primal desire to fulfill my sexual needs instead of wanting to be intimate with them. To be fair, I experienced a couple of flashes of intimacy during my days as a Bachelor but nothing as unique as the bond I have with my Wife.

At the time, the bulk of my experience with intimacy was mostly with my Father. So when I attempted intimacy once again with my Wife, it brought back all the pain and suffering I experienced with my Father. I had difficulties trusting Her touch and often pushed her hands away from me in fear of triggering a mental and physical response. In fact, the flashbacks often caused me to withdraw from physical contact. Over time, with Her gentle persistence, we overcame this obstacle together, and now, none of those triggers affect me. Now that's what love is!

Conditioning can also be associated with habits because you can also condition yourself into doing things that serve you and things that don't, all you need is repetition. Living a healthy lifestyle is something that people can condition themselves into doing. The more they live a healthy lifestyle, the more they condition their brains into wanting to do the activities that are associated with such a lifestyle. The same goes for smoking cigarettes. A person who smokes regularly will eventually condition themselves into smoking every day. To top it off, cigarettes have nicotine in them, which helps solidify their addiction to them. That's why it is so difficult for addicts to quit their drug of choice and for others to maintain a healthy lifestyle. The drug addict becomes addicted to the actual substance in that drug and then gets addicted to the physical act of taking the drug.

To top it off, the addict also gets a shot of dopamine, a chemical that the brain produces to make you feel good. So for the addict, it's like a triple whammy. On the other hand, people who seek to better themselves by eating healthier or exercising don't have a substance to get addicted to per say. They get the shot of dopamine their brains releases into their bodies after they complete the exercise and the endorphins while they exercise. Most importantly, they need to figure out why they want to better themselves physically or mentally. Then they need to continuously will themselves into pursuing better choices, thus creating a better lifestyle. So conditioning is something you repeatedly do until it becomes part of your habitual patterns. Which then becomes part of your normal.

CHAPTER 11

PROGRESSION VS. PERFECTION

Have you ever stopped yourself from learning a new skill? Have you ever dreamed of launching a business but hesitated because you wanted it to be perfect? Do you consider yourself a Perfectionist? Where does the desire to be perfect come from? Does perfection even exist?

The truth is that when we delay our goals due to striving towards perfection, we often don't pursue our goals at all. Based on my experience, the desire to be perfect comes from fear. It's the fear of failure that has often affected how I pursue my own goals. It's the fear that I won't knock it out of the park the first time, which stops me from sharing my gifts. Don't get me wrong, it's OK to have high standards and demand the very best effort from yourself but reaching for perfection is an illusion!!

In addition, saying "You're a perfectionist" is a great way to justify your laziness. It's kind of a cop-out. I've heard people say, and have said this myself, once or twice, "if I can't do it right the first time, I don't want to waste my time." When I said this in the past, it was because I did not want to put in the necessary time it took to master a skill or develop a new ability. The fact is, nothing is perfect, so instead of striving for perfection, focus on progression.

Even George Orwell said:
"The essence of being human is that one does not seek perfection."

If you keep stopping yourself from pursuing your life because of your constant search for perfection, you'll never know what may or may not be right around the corner. For example, I have pursued many careers in various sectors such as Employment, Mining, Construction, Social Services and Customer Service. It is with all that experience that I have come to realize that I enjoy helping people. I also enjoy inspiring people by making inspiring videos. I used to look at my employment history as a colossal failure but have come full circle. I experience no shame with my past employment failures. Being an Employment Counsellor and Life Coach has allowed me to develop my people skills effectively. Having experience in Mining and Construction has allowed me to learn the importance of working hard while being safe. Every failure has a silver lining; all you have to do is look for them. So, if you're thinking about pursuing a particular career, go for it!! You never know what might happen until you give it a go!! The same goes for any other goals you have, think progression and not perfection!

Having said this, I am learning more these days to recognize when I've been beaten. Let me explain. Recently, I pursued a career in HVAC. I thought it would be an excellent opportunity for a new career as I thought I was through with helping people. I was told that I would be making a ton of money and that there would be the possibility of taking over my Student Placement Coordinator's company. So, I went through the schooling and training aspects of a local program. After graduating at the top of my class, I started working for the same company that trained me as a sub-contractor.

At first, I helped the owner install fireplaces on a large scale with the idea of taking over his contracts, and all was going well. We were responsible for installing fireplaces in new construction, and the idea was that I would eventually be doing it all on my own. After a short amount of time, I realized two things. I noticed that the man I was working for reminded me of my Father and not in the right way. He was often condescending towards other people and me, which left a bitter taste in my mouth. He was very confrontational, and in four months, he nearly got into two fights with complete strangers. Also, I realized that I wouldn't be making the kind of money I was promised. What seemed like a fantastic opportunity at first glace quickly deteriorated into a nightmare. The Universe had sent me these signs, among others, and it became clear that the HVAC gig wasn't for me. Don't get me wrong; I could easily do the work and the daily tasks associated with the job, but something inside me was screaming, "This isn't for you!! Get the hell out of here!" I noticed my anxiety and depression levels were rising which increased my anger levels. Simply put, I wasn't really myself! I was becoming like many of the men I was working with, bitter, jaded and miserable. I did not want to become that kind of man at all, so one day after arguing with my boss, again, over a petty issue, I quit! On the spot! So what does this mean?

Well, for me, it's pretty simple. I wasn't quitting because I was striving towards perfection and was failing. In fact, I was mature enough to understand that I would need to progress in the industry if I wanted to become a Master; this was clear to me. It was something else; my heart wasn't into it. It became a drag to go to work, and I really dreaded it. It really stifled my spirit to its core. Deep down, I knew that I was wasting my true talents. I am a Motivator, a Writer, a Story Teller and a Helper. I really like seeing people pull themselves out of their own hell because I understand what it takes to do so. Also, if I can help someone achieve that in any way, that puts me in my element! Sometimes we disguise our laziness with perfection; this is true, but sometimes our heart isn't into what we are doing and being self-aware of this is important. Knowing what is and isn't for you is a sign of maturity. The bottom line is this, forget perfection, think progression and listen to your heart while focusing on what you're already good at! You already have talents that need developing, so don't reinvent the wheel. Focus on what you already have.

Getting started is the only way you can hope to reach your goals. Don't focus too much on whether you're the best at whatever you want to pursue. Instead, focus on becoming the best you can be over time. Make it your life's work! Your LEGACY, if you will! Even if you don't hit it out of the park the first time, by keeping progression in mind, one day you will. Another important point to make is that you would benefit from focusing on what you can do at this moment. It's the small steps that will bring you closer to the next level of your goal. Don't worry too much about the end result. It's good to have a plan, but over-planning can also hinder your progression. It's easy to get overwhelmed or discouraged when looking at the big picture all the time.

It's like trying to pick up all the garbage on the planet; one person can't do this, there's just too much out there! Instead, focus on picking up the trash in your yard or neighbourhood and then progress towards the garbage in your city. Think globally, but act locally because your present self might not be able to handle the magnitude of your desired outcome because you have not grown into the person you need to be to get there...yet. Again, you must focus on developing into your future self by making the best choices in the present moment so that by the time you get to where you wanted to be, you'll be ready.

Think of any Artist, Musician or Athlete you know that is at the top of their game. Did they become successful overnight? Overnight successes rarely happen, if at all. These people got to the top by progressing towards it; they did not fall from the sky only to land on the top of the mountain! They climbed to get there, sometimes on their hands and knees!! Too many people have died and were buried alongside their gifts because they did not take it one step at a time! Instead, they blamed it on the fact that they were perfectionists!!

Robin Sharma said this:

"Slow, steady progress is better than daily excuses."

Please don't let this happen to you! Don't allow yourself to use excuses as reasons why you didn't progress forward. Your light was meant to be seen by everybody, so don't convince yourself that you need to be perfect. Take this book, for example. Even if I have edited it a couple of times, I'm sure there are mistakes here and there that have been overlooked. In fact, I'm counting on it! I know the message in the book is bigger than the few spelling mistakes, so show the world what you're made of, mistakes and all!! Learn from your mistakes while striving towards your goals, take it one day at a time, and eventually, something will come from your efforts.

CHAPTER 12

BEING RIGHT VS. BEING FREE

I was listening to one of Dr. Wayne Dyer's online videos when I heard him say something that really resonated with me. He spoke about life in his usual majestic way and he said:

"When you have the choice between being right and being kind, choose kindness."

Of course this provided me with my own "Ah! Ha!" moment as I immediately thought of my Parents.

As I previously mentioned, over the last few years, I have been on the fence about having a relationship with my parents. When I found out about my Father's continued behaviour a few years ago, it sent me back to when I was a teenager, back in the victim mode. It brought up in me a deep depression and feelings of unworthiness. I kept thinking, "I thought this was over; I thought they moved on?!" My anxiety levels were so bad; I needed to take time off work to rest.

Despite experiencing all these feelings, I eventually decided I would forgive them for their shortcomings in an attempt to rekindle our fragile relationship. My decision to do so even prompted our move back to our hometown, where my parents resided. I thought things would be different, I thought they had changed, but I was wrong! People don't change. People can change things about themselves if they put in the effort, but as soon as the effort goes away, they usually revert to being who they once were. The best example of this is when you look at someone who has lost a bunch of weight. When they follow their plan, they maintain their progress. As soon as they fall off the wagon for an extended period of time, they usually put the weight back on.

When we moved to Ottawa, I decided that I would continue to forgive them from a distance. You see, when I am away from them, I strive. I put in the work to better myself and strive towards the dreams and goals I want to accomplish, but that all falls apart when I have them in my life. One of the reasons is because I don't feel like they validate me, like they don't see me for who I am now but see me for who I was as a child and teenager. I also revert to that role when I am with them. I wanted to work on our relationship, and they did not. "Your Father has done his time," is a statement that I have heard them say on several occasions. Especially when the conversation heads towards the healing, growth and development of our family dynamic. It's another way of saying, "Don't go there!"

I also feel like they don't support me; in fact, when speaking to my Mother about the personal development industry, my blog and the motivational videos I was making, she said, "You know, your Father and I aren't really into all that feel-good stuff!" Which is another way of saying, "We don't really care about what you're doing!" Even though I don't feel validated and supported by them, I do feel the need to forgive them continuously. I just can't have them in my life.

Marianne Williamson said this about forgiveness:
"Forgiveness is a process, and it doesn't mean the person we forgive will necessarily be our friend—for a while, or ever. If you've done something awful to me or to someone I love, I don't see myself hanging out and having lunch with you anytime soon."

Like the person losing or gaining weight, I am at my best when I am on my wagon. Unfortunately, my parents are not sitting beside me. Now, I think about what Dr. Wayne Dyer said, and I understand what he was saying now more than ever. By distancing myself from them, I am kind to them and myself instead of trying to convince myself that everything is alright. I am kind towards them because I am not trying to convince them that they need changing and kind to myself by realizing my own self-worth. I'm through with chasing them, and as much as it saddens me, I know it is for the best. I deserve better, my Wife and Daughter deserve better, and even my parents deserve better!

I realized that we all live within the limits of our own thoughts and that challenging someone's reality can be difficult, if not futile. You see, I got so caught up in the drama of being right that I forgot that being kind would free me. I don't have to have them in my life to be able to forgive them. I totally accept them for who they are, and even if I don't agree with how they live their lives, it is with that acceptance that I free myself.

As I said before, it's hard to change someone because change must come from within, and no matter how hard we try to convince them, we will never change their mind. Being kind through forgiveness isn't something I am doing for them. No, in fact, I do for myself and my inner peace! I am not holding on to the grudge I had when in their presence because I wanted them to change, and they didn't see the need. I am free of that now, truly free! Sometimes, the best thing you can do for a relationship is end it.

Ending the relationship further helped me move towards forgiveness. Isn't that interesting?? My parents would never be the parents I wanted them to be because my perception of what they should be like was part of MY reality, not THEIRS. In fact, the parents I want are long gone and may never be seen again, and that's OK, that belongs to them. I also must consider that they feel and think the same way about me. We're not to be frightened by this two-way street of give and take. In fact, it is with this realization that I have come full circle in accepting my parents for who they are in their as-is state.

CHAPTER 13

CELEBRATE YOUR LIFE'S VICTORIES

Overall, I don't think we celebrate our lives and the victories we experience enough. Life is truly a celebration, and rejoicing is the fuel that keeps us going. It is easy to be zoned out into our daily routines, but if we don't shake things up once and a while, life can get pretty stagnant, causing us to miss the subtle beauty life has to offer!

Ferris Bueller describes this beautifully:
"Life moves pretty fast. If you don't stop and look around once in a while, you could miss it."

Let's face it, other than our birthdays, holidays, and the odd occasion that our favourite sports team wins something, we don't celebrate all that much. Think about it for a second…when do you celebrate? It's almost like we are programmed to celebrate only when society deems it to be appropriate. I don't want to confuse celebrating with partying as they are different.

With the help of Uncle Google, let me define the

difference between the two: "Partying is when you enjoy yourself at a party or other lively gathering, typically with drinking and music. Celebrating is to publicly acknowledge (a significant or happy day or event) with a social gathering or enjoyable activity." I think the main thing to retain here is that you can party for no reason, but celebrating is usually attached to something special, like weddings, birthdays, or job promotions. Having said this, celebrating doesn't have to be that elaborate, it can be as simple as seeing the sunrise with your significant other or hearing the rainfall on a tin roof while you lay in your warm and cozy bed. Celebrations can be about the little things in life and don't necessarily have to be reserved for big occasions.

While attending the Unleash the Power Within Seminar, Tony Robbins made the same observation and often had us celebrate. At first, it felt very unnatural as he would literally tell us to jump up and down to celebrate things that didn't warrant much celebrating. At least that's what it seemed like at first. He would make us celebrate someone else's breakthrough. He would encourage us to celebrate someone making a great point. As we progressed, I realized that celebrating these things was super important. It invited more great moments in my life and also encouraged people to contribute more during the seminar. It was showing me that I needed to celebrate things that I usually took for granted, such as life!

When was the last time you celebrated being alive, besides your birthday? When was the last time you celebrated the fact that you were born a human and not an ant or a slug? The odds of being a human are very low; in fact, with an estimated 1 trillion different lifeforms on this planet, you were miraculously born a human! Think about that for a moment! Now CELEBRATE!!

Another thing you could celebrate is the fact that you're alive and reading this book right now! Celebrating the fact that you woke up this morning can really ground you in the present moment. It will make you feel grateful for being alive. If you can start your day by celebrating the fact that you made it through the night and are alive to live on for one more day, you will have given yourself a head start!

Even Oprah Winfrey said:
"The more you celebrate your life, the more there is in life to celebrate."

How true is that? This is one of the breakthroughs I continue to develop and hope you will consider it as part of your life too. Celebrating your victories will program your brain into wanting more of what's making you feel great. If you are attempting to quit smoking and you've just completed your first day smoke free...celebrate! If you said no to that yummy chocolate cake at work and opted for a healthy alternative...celebrate! If you are progressing towards your own business and have connected with a new client...celebrate! Celebrate! Celebrate!!

There is much to celebrate in this world, so start living it up, you deserve it and are worthy of it! You can celebrate just about anything BTW. My Wife and I celebrate things like doing yoga and meditation sessions together, usually with a high five or a kiss. Or sometimes, we'll go crazy by jumping around while laughing in our kitchen. After our morning Live Facebook Feeds, we celebrate with a passionate high-five!!

Personally, in those moments, I truly feel happy and have an overall sense of inner peace and that, in itself, is worth celebrating!

CHAPTER 14

TIME, WHERE HAVE YOU GONE?

With the awareness of the Universe's age as it is compared to time, we don't live very long. We think we do, but in all reality, we don't. We live for just a brief moment, most of us living in two states of mind. Either we live in the past, or we live in the future. The past harbours feelings of regret, guilt, self-judgment, anger and depression. While the future holds anxiety, uncertainty, worry and fear, which governs most of our decisions, often paralyzing us.

What we don't realize, at least, what I didn't know was by living this way, I forgot that there was this ever-fleeting moment that I was missing. Caught up in the past and future, I didn't even know what the present moment was. Often lost in my head, I would miss what was happening right in front of me. Living in those two states of mind shaped my personality. Living in a state of anger, sadness and depression because of thoughts about my past and fear and anxiety because of thoughts about my future.

When I realized that the future and the past don't

really exist, I started living more in the present moment. As concepts, the past and future exist, but only when we put our energy there. When we focus on our past or the potential of our future, we bring them to life through our thoughts. When we focus only on the present moment, the past and future disappear. I actually experienced peace, real peace, when in the present moment. To elaborate on this further, because our past is behind us, it actually doesn't exist anymore. The only reason it exists in our minds is because we have chosen to save or to hold on to it. Much like a computer, our brain has the power of retaining any of the past experiences we have witnessed by choosing to hold on to them. I used to hold on to all the negative memories that I experienced, and because I focused on them a lot, they overshadowed many of the good memories I experienced.

I had to reboot my memory!! Focusing on all the great memories of my past brought more great memories forward for me to see. Even if I drift off from time to time, I focus mostly on living within the now. The same goes for living in the future, it doesn't exist, so why get lost in the "what if this happens?" kind of mentality. Planning for your future is essential, but getting lost living there won't serve you. Living in the future didn't do me any justice, and at some point, you just have to let go and know that things will work themselves out. When I used to think of the future, I would imagine myself being this great man, with all this money. I'd be helping others while living a lavish life, and when reality set in, it would depress the hell out of me because my vision seemed unattainable. Mostly unattainable because of my faulty thinking and bad habits.

For some reason the pattern would start again, and I would dive into living in the future while the present moment drifted away. I realized that I could be that fantastic guy in the present, and if I worked hard enough, the future life I imagined and wanted so much would eventually come true. We are the total sum of all our thoughts, so if you always think about how bad your past was, the odds are that the future will bring more of the same. Which will undoubtedly continue your self-defeating prophecy. Another way of looking at it is, attention goes where energy flows. Where you spend your time is very important!

J. R. R. Tolkien said it well when he said:
"All we have to decide is what to do with the time that is given us."

Simply put, it doesn't matter how much time you have to live here on this planet. What matters is what you do with the time you have. Whether it's 39 or 109 years, use your time wisely!

My pursuit of development allowed me to realize that time and life is short. It forced me into becoming the person I wanted to be, the person I was meant to be in the present moment. I realized that my happiness wasn't dependent on some future event or happening but, in fact, dependent on what I did in the present moment. The choices I made on a day to day basis would either bring me closer to my dream or distance me further from it.

As time passed, like it usually does, I started thinking about how many years I have left here on earth, and it was either when I was listening to "The Power of Now" by Eckhart Tolle or "I Can See Clearly Now" by Dr. Wayne Dyer that I learned something valuable. I learned that time, which is man-made, is an illusion and that I don't have a specific number of years left to experience certain things but, in fact, a specific number of times to experience certain things.

Let me explain this a little more in-depth, one of these Teachers suggested that we think about the number of times we have left to do certain things instead of counting the years we have left to do it. It really puts things in perspective, doesn't it? This way of thinking really hit home for me as it had me thinking about some of the events I experience yearly. Specifically, our yearly XMAS get together with friends. After thinking about it, I realized that I don't have X number of years left to experience this event, but instead, X number of times left to experience this.

Let that sink in for a second. Have you thought about how many times you have left to experience Summer? Or how many times you have left to go on your yearly family vacation? Of course, thinking this way can be depressing, if that's how you take it. I feel very grateful for all the moments I have experienced so far, including the good, bad, and ugly. These moments have taught me many lessons that have moulded me into the man that I am now and the man that I continuously aim to be.

Thinking this way has also provided me with a sense of urgency which keeps telling me to do something with passion and purpose, and furthermore, it reminds me of how important it is to surround myself with great friends and family. More importantly, it encourages me to make more of an effort to see them more as I appreciate them in my life.

The bottom line is that life is much shorter than it seems, and we must see the present moment for what it really is, a gift. Life is too short to feel like crap all the time! You are not your thoughts, so please avoid living in your past or future emotional states. Feel what you have to feel and then move on!

CHAPTER 15

LEGACY VS. EMOTIONAL BAGGAGE

Now that I have a family of my own, I have learned a few things that are imperative to my Daughter's well-being and development. Through the book "The Conscious Parent," written by Dr. Shefali Tsabary, I have learned that I have to strive towards passing down my Legacy as opposed to my Emotional Baggage. It is one of the keys to her future success in life!

Another interesting quote I read from Frederick Douglass states this:
"It is easier to build strong children than to repair broken adults."

How true is that?? Building an excellent foundation for your child's future development and growth is so important! Personally, I think that my parents did the best they could even though they weren't conscious enough to build my Brother and me up as children. I'm coming from a place of observation and not resentment. They didn't really know how because they weren't raised that way by their parents.

My parents even talked about how their parents never told them to follow their dreams or pursue something they enjoyed doing. That kind of talk wasn't really as mainstream as it is in today's world. The speech they got, which they gave us, was something like "get good grades, so you can get a good job, so you can pay your bills" or a variation of something like that.

Did you get that message? Or did your parents tell you to shoot for the moon? Did you follow your passion and strive towards your dreams? Or did you get good grades to get a good job to pay your bills? As parents, we need to teach our children to become more than just "bill payers." We need to show them that it's OK to shoot for the stars!

As mentioned in a previous chapter, I believe that we tend to inherit more of our family's lifestyle than genetics. With that said, I think that we inherit some of our parents' behaviours and attitudes and some of their parenting styles. What I got from them, they got from their parents and so on and so forth. This is good if the lifestyle you're inheriting comes from kindness, compassion, adventure, wisdom and honesty. If not, you might get stuck with your parents' baggage because they received it from their parents, and then passed it onto you. Thus continuing the cycle of mediocrity.

A prime example of this is when poor parents tell their children that money doesn't bring happiness. As much as there is some truth to that, it's not the whole truth. Sure, money can't buy you happiness, but it sure can provide you with freedom of choice. Don't want to drive an old unreliable car? Money helps buy you an excellent reliable vehicle. Don't want to live in the Ghetto? Money can help you live somewhere nicer. This message that money can't buy you happiness is the message I got at home, so I never put value on money when I should have thought about money in a different way. This is one of the reasons, I have been poor!

Grant Cardone knows what he's talking about:
"Money can't buy you happiness, but being broke can't either!"

No parent is perfect, and that applies to all parents, even myself. Parents make mistakes, and that's normal. We can only develop our parenting skills over time in hopes that our children grow into well-adjusted human beings. To me, parenthood is not the act of striving for perfection but a journey of self-discovery, self-love, and progress.

All we can do is be self-aware of what worked for our parents, what didn't work and make the corrections needed to evolve as conscious parents. Too often, people raised in an environment where the parents are depressed, anxious, and on medication tend to take on their parents' emotional baggage. It's like they become carbon copies of their parents. We hear this often when people say stuff like "she's just like her dad, or he's becoming more and more like his grandfather." The same goes for what I went through as a child and teenager. Being raised in my environment forced me to adopt patterns of anger, anxiety, and depression, leading to feelings of self-worthlessness.

My Father belittled us often, sometimes without

knowing it, and it left many marks on my spirit. It doesn't surprise me that I adopted a similar behaviour towards my Wife and Daughter. I work hard at not being that way, and even if I know that I am doing better than I once was, I slip often. It's not on purpose and will often happen when I am not being present. As I focus on being present, my negative behaviour seems to melt away. My Father was blunt in his approach, and I have also adopted this into my personality. I will often speak without adding kindness or compassion to my words, and in return, I hurt the people I love. I own this! I know I can be this way, and I am working towards developing myself. I admit these are not my best traits, but I also enjoy entertaining people by making them laugh, which is another family trait. With my development in mind, I have learned to accept myself for who I am, in my as-is state! That's where growth and development starts!!

Having said this, I understand the importance of changing my negative patterns because of the long-lasting effects they will have on my Daughter. Children will subconsciously learn from their parents' behaviour, so all I can say to you is be careful what you choose to say and do to your children as you have no idea what kind of impact you're having on them. When they say kids are like sponges, that's a lie! They're more like sponges on steroids! They know when you're being funny, and even when you're being disingenuous. They are wise beyond their years, and we can all learn from children, all we have to do is pay attention!!

Dr. Seuss made this significant observation:
"A person's a person, no matter how small!"

Trust in children's kindness, compassion and honesty and remember that your child is learning new things all the time and will make mistakes. Teach them that it's OK to make mistakes and that they can learn valuable lessons from them. Even if your child isn't as developed or as grown as you are, they can still be your teachers. Don't be afraid to learn from them as well, I know I have.

In fact, one event that sticks out in my mind is when my Daughter taught me a valuable lesson about letting go. We were walking around our local Farmers' Market when my Daughter, who was 4-5 years old at the time, wanted to play in the central water fountain. She asked me if she could go into the water to splash around, and my gut feeling was to say no, which I did initially. Not because I didn't want her to play, but because I did not want to draw attention towards myself as I might feel embarrassed or judged. Against my gut feeling, I decided to let her do her thing and observed with amazement at the reaction I saw from others.

Nobody looked at us with hate or anger but instead looked at us with joy. Furthermore, nobody was looking at me, they were focused on her. It was like I could see these people living vicariously through my Daughter as they wished they were the ones playing in the fountain. I noticed smiles everywhere, even from across the street! I looked as they marvelled at my Daughter's playful ways. I realized that letting go of my own insecurities allowed so many people to feel joy and happiness. I also realized that my Daughter has her own path to walk and that her journey won't always include me and that I am not to be frightened by that. I need to trust that she'll know where to go and what to do when the time comes. It is within moments like these that letting go allows us to truly flourish.

If we listen and watch our children, they can be our gurus!! All we have to do is let go of the idea that we are superior because we are older and that we know better. Age doesn't equal wisdom. We can all benefit from letting go of the need to have so many imaginary rules, hindering our growth. My Daughter has provided me with inspiring and teachable moments and amazes me with her delight! A real Angel sent to us from Source to guide us towards healing!

Dr. Wayne Dyer said this:
"Parents are not for leaning upon, but rather exist to make leaning unnecessary."

CHAPTER 16

FEAR HOLDING YOU BACK?

Does fear stop you from living the life you want? I was listening to Mastin Kipp's audio book "Daily Love: Growing into Grace," and what he said about fear was very interesting.

He talks about how if you want to live a fearless life, you'd better stay in your comfort zone. I'm not sure if he coined it or if he was quoting somebody else, the source is irrelevant. What I think he meant was, sometimes our fear is debilitating and can stop us from experiencing life in all its wonder. The flip side is fear can also be a great tool when striving for growth or when attempting to reach a goal. We will all experience some form of fear at one point in our lives, and we can either allow it to cripple us or use it to empower us!

Ask yourself this: Do I want to simply survive, or do I want to thrive? People who tend to live in survival mode don't take many chances and are quick to settle in many aspects of their lives. These people often complain about not liking their work, relationships, and even their health but rarely do anything about it because it isn't their fault. Rarely do these people take ownership of their lives/choices and, as a default, blame others for their misfortune. These people often can't control their own fear and are ruled by it, which hinders them from experiencing their full potential.

As I write this chapter, I can't help but think about myself. I lived a life filled with fear and feared what people might think of me. I thought this way so much that I felt paralyzed. Afraid of sharing my talents and authentic self, I stayed hidden in the corner of my own mind, a prisoner of sorts, if you will. I blamed my Father for my misfortunes and lack of success, and I often settled for opportunities that left me feeling like I was wasting my time. I repeated this pattern over and over until one day, I realized that it's OK to put value in what others might think of you, as long as you take it all with a grain of salt! Never forget that fear can be debilitating, and even if this is true, fear can also be used as a guide to help us grow while striving for our full potential.

People who thrive, see life as basically a series of choices and that as individuals, we have total control over our choices, in fact, it's all we can control. These people see a bad situation and make it good. They see a good situation and make it great, and they see that same great situation and make it blissful. I'm not saying that life is all rainbows and butterflies because people who strive still experience hardship and failure. That's part of life!! The main difference is that they learn from their mistakes or unfortunate circumstances in order to move forward. They work through their fear using it as a guide and not as a crutch, and with that, comes a life filled with bliss, happiness and fulfillment. I have been chipping away at my rough edges for a long time now, and it used to get me down. I felt like I should be a different person while missing the fact that I was already enough, which helped me strive towards becoming another person. A person that feared a little less and loved more.

Robin Sharma said this:
"The fears we don't face, become our limits!"

As humans, we will spend a part of our lives experiencing fear, and there's not much we can do to change that. What we can do though, is decide whether the fear we experience is happening to us or happening for us. If we chose the attitude that "it's happening to us" we are left playing the victim's role. Victims often feel helpless because they haven't seized control of their life which perpetuates their cycle of victimization. On the other hand, if we chose the attitude of "it's happening for us," we can realize that we are meant to learn from the experience instead of being controlled by it. If you believe that life happens for you, you will start to see that every day is part of the continuous apprenticeship we call life!

I have often asked myself, can my fear drive me into being a better person? I have come to the conclusion that it really can. Running from my fears never worked for me, it actually made things worse. Instead of pursuing something that I enjoyed, I found myself making up excuses for why I couldn't do them, which ultimately stifled my spirit even further. When you deny your soul or inner being the emotions it gets from doing something it enjoys, I believe it dies a little. I often denied myself the joys I got when I played with my guitar while singing a couple of tunes. I was afraid that I wouldn't be perfect or the best, and it stopped me dead in my tracks. For years, my guitar stayed in its case, never seeing the light of day. Now, I have it displayed on a stand where I can see it as a daily reminder to pick it up and jam, just jam! The guitar is also visible as a reminder to pursue other talents instead of keeping them in cases somewhere, never to be shared.

Now, I challenge myself by heading towards my fears, and the results have been positive. We have all been fearful of not performing well at some point. Whether it's related to sports, music, art, careers or love, our fears drive us. Having said this, only we can decide where they drive us. Will they drive us towards a life worth living, or will they enslave us? The choice is ours!! Our fears have the potential of pushing us towards training harder, studying more, being a better version of ourselves and loving more. So the next time you're about to deny your spirit from bliss by running away from your fear, head towards the other direction. Instead of seeking security, seek adventure!! I promise you'll never look back!! Besides, nobody has ever accomplished greatness from the comfort of their couch, you gotta get up and push yourself beyond the fear!

CHAPTER 17

HATERS BE CRAZY!

It has occurred to me that no matter how much good one strives to achieve, there will always be haters or people who don't understand your vision. Their lack of vision will cause them to undermine you or even try to break you down.

It doesn't matter what you say or do either, because their egos won't allow them to see past themselves. I speak from experience here because I was one of those haters. I would see someone post something on Facebook, and because I felt like shit, I often used sarcasm to tear down what they were saying even if their message was positive. I would disguise my self-hatred with smart and witty jabs I used to punch people with all because I didn't like myself. I would also manipulate people into feeling guilty for not thinking the way I thought. This clash of opinions was caused as a direct result of me letting my ego drive my behaviour, and it almost cost me a few friends and even my marriage.

Looking back, I realize that I did this because I didn't feel good about myself and because I was jealous of their happiness. I wanted them to be as miserable as I was. You can't spread love towards others if you don't have it for yourself. Now that I've changed my ways, I think the best way to deal with haters is to not allow them to pull you into their vortex of misery, which can be very difficult.

Will Smith once said:
"Haters are the people who will broadcast your failures and whisper your success!"

Having said this, I foolishly allowed myself to engage in a conversation with a hater, and it completely drained me emotionally and physically. It was on Mother's Day, and I had sent a post on Facebook about how grateful I was to have my Wife by my side and that I was lucky to have her. We were sitting outside, the sun was shining, and we were really enjoying Mother's Day as a family. My phone notified me about an incoming comment, and I felt the urge to look at it. At the time, I wasn't in contact with my parents and the comment came from a hater, from my Father's side of the family, who felt like it was her duty to tell me how much I should appreciate my Mother because at least, my Mother was still alive.

I agreed with the hater because I knew her Mother had passed and stated that I was grateful that my Mother was healthy. This wasn't enough for the hater as she continued to lecture me about how I should live my life. My replies were answered with back-handed and passive-aggressive comments, and what seemed to be an innocent exchange of words quickly turned into an online argument. I got all bent out of shape because, again, no matter what I said or how I said it, the hater didn't want to consider my side.

Instead of backing off, we spend our time and energy running around in circles, arguing over something that wasn't even her business, to begin with. To be fair, I get where she was coming from being that her Mom was gone and all, I just think that her intention was misguided as we did not share the same circumstances. First of all, she could not speak to her Mother because she had passed away, and I wasn't talking to my Mother because they lied to us about my Father's latest escapade. Two very different scenarios, all of which were explained to the hater without success.

They say Karma's a bitch, and I can't help but think that Karma was there that day to teach me a valuable lesson. I was now aware of how hurtful I had been towards my friends through Social Media. The pain and turmoil I was experiencing during this useless conversation with my hater were probably felt by the people I sucked into pointless discussions in the past. To be quite honest, I am so happy and grateful that I learned from my mistake. Otherwise, I would have never moved forward and probably would still be making useless comments online!! So, thank you very much, Karma!

I have to admit that at first, I felt anger towards this person. I couldn't grasp why she wasn't getting what I was saying, and I couldn't believe how she was replying to me!

The anger I felt was short-lived as I understood that this person was probably dealing with their own issues and insecurities, just like I was when I was an online hater. I actually felt much more compassion towards that person because of the whole conversation. I get how difficult and draining it can be to have your ego drive your behaviour. Been there!! Done that!! If we were honest with ourselves and with everyday people, we might allow our inner selves to shine through all the nonsense caused by our insecurities.

Some people will always attempt to destroy the progress you've been working towards, especially when it doesn't align with their values and lifestyle. It's very similar to when you plant a garden. As soon as you're done the planting and watering, the weeds come out to invade your garden, and if you don't work in your garden, the weeds will take it! People aren't necessarily weeds, but they might be fearful of losing you and subconsciously feel the need to drag you back down to their comfort level.

One thing you must consider when seeking growth or a lifestyle change is that not everyone around you is doing the same, and that's OK. The most important thing to remember is, don't let the opinions of haters discourage you from achieving your happiness, no matter what.

Steve Maraboli states that:
"If you fuel your journey on the opinions of others, you are going to run out of gas!"

This is why I place so much importance on who I surround myself with. These people have to be supportive and understanding of my goal/vision. In fact, the more you'll strive towards your goals, despite the haters, the more you will find like-minded people who will support and encourage you. I hope you find these people!!

CHAPTER 18

WHAT IS HAPPINESS?

Since I started my personal growth, I told myself that I would never stop seeking the truth about who I truly am. I know that it's my responsibility to generate my own happiness and that it really is **you vs. you** in this life. I think it's important to seek personal growth because if you're not growing, ultimately, you're dying!

As mentioned in a previous chapter, I watched the documentary by Tom Shadyac "I Am" (2011) on Netflix, and it really opened my eyes to an inconvenient truth we all live with. This truth has us brainwashed into thinking that we must separate ourselves from the general population to stand out so that we can reach success—kind of an everybody vs. everybody mentality. This truth has us believing that the word success is somehow attached to how much money or stuff you have.

In the movie, they talk about the truth and the lie around the happiness we get from owning stuff. I will paraphrase their example as best I can. Imagine you were in the woods, naked, lost and in the middle of a winter storm. We can all agree that your happiness level probably wouldn't be very high, to say the least. Now, as you helplessly tried to find your bearings, you stumbled across a small cabin where the owner welcomed you in, offering warm shelter, clothing and something to eat. The truth is, you would most likely feel a lot happier because of the items you have just received. True? Are you still with me?? Now the lie leads you to believe that if you feel great owning 10 items, how much more joy would you experience if you had 20 items? What about 50 items? Or 100?

Audrey Hepburn had this to say about happiness:
"The most important thing is to enjoy your life - to be happy. It's all that matters!"

Marketing experts have been plaguing us with this lie for a long time, confusing us to believe that happiness is the equivalent of being greedy and that having lots of stuff is what success is all about. They also confuse us by convincing us that the more we buy things for others, the more they'll think that we love them. They also play the other hand by telling us that we must receive gifts to feel loved. Haven't you noticed that most holidays are now focused on gift buying? They concentrate on making you feel guilty so that you'll think you don't have a choice in buying gifts for everyone, even if at the expense of your credit.

The truth is simple, happiness comes from within and is not something you can fake by obtaining more stuff. In fact, the rush we feel from getting stuff is usually short-lived, leaving us with the same void and emptiness we were trying to fill in the first place. This creates a never-ending cycle of consumerism. Tom even mentions it in the film. He had all this stuff and still felt like it wasn't enough, like something was missing. He had cars, private jets, a mansion filled with stuff only rich people can buy and yet, he felt empty. He had more money than he knew what to do with and he still was unhappy. I will admit that I used to fall for this trap because of the constant bombardment of ads and propaganda. I used to get myself into debt by buying gifts for this person or that person, all while worrying about how I would pay off my newly acquired debt.

We all have our own definition of happiness, which is based on many factors. Where you were raised, who raised you, your friends, your love life, and your career path are just a few of these factors. You can quickly figure out whether you're happy by thinking about the satisfaction you feel from the overall quality of your life, plus how good you're going to feel from day to day. If you like your overall life and feel good on average, it would be safe to assume that you live a happy life. One of the things I do to elevate my level of happiness is to practice daily gratitude. Upon waking up, I thank the Universe for giving me one more day! Another kick at the can if you will!! Grateful people experience more joy because they tend to appreciate what they already have as opposed to stressing about what they don't. I know people who own houses with attached garages that are not used for housing cars. Instead, the garage is filled with stuff!! Things they use on occasion, things they use once a year and things they can't get rid of because "you never know when you might need that thingamajig." It's madness! These are the same people who keep adding more stuff, year after year, after year!!

The wise Buddha nailed it with this one:
"*There is no path to happiness: happiness is the path!*"

People who practice gratitude regularly don't feel the need to clutter their lives with useless stuff. My Wife and I experienced this first hand when we decided to move back to our home town. We thought a new start, in a new place, would help us transition to the next stage of our lives. Most people wait until they're old to downsize, and we thought we'd get a head start by selling our home while moving into an apartment. We wanted to downsize, and part of that was getting rid of stuff. We were just like everyone else. We had too much stuff, most of it we didn't even use. It was just there creating clutter in our house and clutter in our minds. Did you know the more stuff you have, the more anxious you feel? One of the reasons is that your subconscious mind keeps track of all your stuff.

We sold our three-bedroom home and sold more than half of our stuff. What we could not sell, we gave away. I actually gave away most of my power tools to Syrian Refugees who were coming to Canada. My Wife donated half of our linens to a charity for women and children. Initially, we were both reluctant to sell our stuff, let alone give it away!! Seriously! We had major reservations towards the whole process! Many people identify themselves with the things they own like it's a badge of honour or something like that. We were no different!! Here's what surprised me; once we started selling stuff and the house started feeling emptier and emptier, I became less and less anxious, and so did my Wife. I started caring less about stuff and liked being light and able to go anywhere without worrying about my stuff. This was so surreal that we almost got addicted to getting rid of our stuff. It's what actually prompted me into giving all of my power tools away!! I knew I wouldn't need them where we were moving, and I could always buy more if needed. Besides, I kept the essential hand tools and kits, and it's not like stores were going to stop selling tools anytime soon!!

Nathaniel Hawthorne once said:
"Happiness is not found in the things you possess, but in what you have the courage to release."

Another thing you can do to help elevate your happiness levels is to help others. Do something beautiful for a stranger or the next-door neighbour. When we help others, it makes us feel good because we know we are doing a good deed. Humans were made to serve others, and that's why it feels so good when we do. To further build on this thought, your brain actually releases Oxytocin when you bond socially with someone. Oxytocin is so powerful that it is even released when you witness someone being nice! That's right!! Just seeing someone being nice gives you a shot of Oxytocin! Oxytocin is a hormone that is often called the love hormone. I think we could all benefit from being more Oxytocin-like.

Even the Beatles had a hit song called "All You Need is Love." You don't have to reinvent the wheel when it comes to helping others, it's actually pretty simple. Bring in your neighbour's empty garbage cans from the street, shovel their driveway(if applicable), cut their grass or make them a home-cooked meal. You don't have to buy anyone a car or a trip to Disneyland, keep it simple!! If doing something physical for your neighbour isn't possible, due to whatever reason, start by saying hello when you see them. Engage them in a friendly conversation; it's that simple!!

There are plenty of things you can do to elevate your level of happiness. As I am writing this, we are in the middle of the 2020 Covid-19 Pandemic. During these times, staying happy is the most important thing. We have been self-isolating for about 12 weeks, and we have made a valiant effort to pursue happiness. One of the things we have done is set up a video conference with our friends where we play dice and chat about the usual nonsense. It's like an online party! We actively connect with the ones we love to nurture our relationships because we don't know when this is going to end and are planning for the long haul. Even if we can't see each other in person, video conferencing is the next best thing, and I am genuinely grateful for the technology we have at our fingertips. Imagine if this pandemic happened before the internet!

Speaking of technology, my Wife and I have started doing a Live Feed through Facebook. We have been consistent with our daily shows, and we are enjoying the time we collaborate together. In fact, we have realized that we make a great on-screen team, and because of this, we have decided to pursue an online business where we help people through free content, online training, books and live events. I think it's important to try new things because you never know what can come from them. Plus, when you complete something new, your brain releases Dopamine because of the sense of accomplishment you feel. Trying new things is incredible and won't kill you, so give it a go! You never know what will happen!

CHAPTER 19

KEYBOARD WARRIORS

The Internet and its sense of anonymity have created a bunch of self-entitled assholes. We've all seen Keyboard Warriors say things from the comfort of their couches that they would never say to anybody's face. I watch YouTube videos, probably too many of them, and it never ceased to amaze me how quickly the comment section becomes a combat zone of insults and small-minded rhetoric.

It never seems to matter what kind of videos I'm watching; the comment section always ends up in some sort of battle between two opinions—often becoming a debate about religion, politics, black lives matter, all lives matter and everything in between. Some people do it on purpose. They go out seeking conflict, in hopes of finding people to belittle and trash. They do this so much that they have been dubbed "Online Trolls." For some reason, these people purposely bait others with conversation only to turn everything on its head, causing conflict.

There used to be a time when you could have a civil

disagreement with someone without the conversation going to hell!! Debates where both parties came to common ground or get to a point where they agreed to disagree. These stalemates were often met with a pint and a chuckle, but now those times seem to be long gone!! In today's world of triggered people, if you disagree with someone's opinion or point of view, you are thrown into the pit of endless labels, where you can be left blacklisted and even unemployed! I have seen people who are supporters of specific groups get called the exact opposite of who they are and what they stand for! All because they questioned some of their group's values, intentions and didn't agree 100% with what they stood for. It's gotten to the point where Online Trolls will go back through all of your social media platforms to search for something that isn't Politically Correct, just to tear you down!

This Cancel Culture even went after the famous Comedian, and Actor Kevin Hart when he was asked to host the 2019 Oscars. It was his dream to host the Oscars!! The Trolls went back to find something that he posted ten years prior only to tarnish his name, and they succeeded! They found decade-old homophobic tweets made by Kevin Hart and demanded an apology. He eventually said he was sorry and that he didn't mean to hurt anyone. Even fellow Comedian Dave Chappelle said that Hart is "as close to perfect as anybody I've ever seen," but is "precisely four tweets shy" of being faultless. All that to say that Kevin did not host the Oscars. Kevin even went on to say that he was evolving and wanted to continue to do so. If a person says they're sorry and acknowledges they made a mistake, it should be the end of it! Isn't it human to make mistakes? I make a handful of mistakes every day, but I learn from them and evolve because of them.

This quote by Benjamin Franklin sums it up for me:
"Without freedom of thought there can be no such thing as wisdom; and no such thing as public liberty, without freedom of speech."

It's even goes further than that! For some reason, some people like to think that their opinions are worth more than the facts of another. Some people will argue the hell out of their views without offering any facts, and that can be dangerous!! Specifically if the person has an online following! People think that who they follow are extensions of their personalities and often take on the opinions of these "Influencers" as their own. This phenomenon can be beneficial if the "Influencer" is of sound mind, but might not work out if the "Influencer's" thinking is off the rails.

To add to this, algorithms make decisions or recommendations that point us towards the information we are looking for when we search for a specific thing or subject. The algorithms also keep pushing what you searched for, even after you've stopped looking to personalize the Internet for every user. Have you ever noticed when you search for, let's say a car, the ads you see after are often of the vehicle you were looking up or at least, the type of car you were looking for or a local car dealership? Well, that's what an algorithm does, it sort of puts you in a vacuum or bubble and all you can see is what you search for, even after you've moved on to something else. This is a problem because it can isolate you from opposing arguments or points of view and can actually exacerbate your own biases. We are not to be frightened by algorithms, but we need to be aware of what they're doing to avoid being sucked into the vacuum.

Here's the thing, the Internet is both equally a good and a bad thing. You can find all sorts of learning tutorials online from piano playing, Math lessons or how to fix whatever. You can keep in touch with family or friends through video chat and even shop from the comfort of your own house. As always, where there is good, there will also be bad to counter its effects, to bring balance. The Yin and Yang!! We, the operators of the web, have a great responsibility. We must govern ourselves towards being champions of kindness and compassion as opposed to becoming Internet Trolls.

In a previous chapter, I explained how I was one of these "Trolls" at one point. I would play mind games with others only to make myself feel superior and smart, but the results were always the same, I felt empty. I was jealous of others' happiness, and my only response was to tear them down with insults and sarcasm. I bet these Trolls feel like I did…empty!

On Facebook, I have also noticed people playing the victim and with their statuses go off blaming others for why they feel a certain way. They call out others who have "done them wrong" without ever looking within themselves to consider their part. Week after week, new statuses come in blaming this one or that one for their unhappiness. It's really quite sad! They can't even own their misery!! It's always somebody else's fault!! Then you have the complainers who complain about this and complain about that. They're always coming from the perception that life is so hard for them, and if we could only spend a day in their shoes, we would understand. Always bitching about stuff that is happening to them and how life isn't fair!

Life isn't fair, and that is something we all have an equal share in! Bad luck or bad things aren't reserved for a specific group of people; they happen to us all. As I mentioned before, a real sign of maturity is when someone takes full responsibility for their life, without blame or complaint. They own it, and that's what makes them an adult. That's what it means to be a grownup!! To take ownership of your life can only do one thing, empower you!! Pretending that an external force is responsible for your happiness level will only strip you of your power! Don't do it!!

CHAPTER 20

CHOOSING EXCITEMENT OVER ANXIETY

Have you ever been on a roller coaster? Imagine yourself tightly strapped in one, and as you're being pulled up the initial incline, you hear the familiar sound of click, click, click!!! Once atop, the mechanism releases and for a brief moment, the train gently coasts before it rushes down the rails at top speed!! Whoosh! Have you ever noticed how some people put their hands in the air while others hold on tightly? Why do you think people do that? Why do some hold on tightly while others let go freely?

Are you the type of person that let's go, or are you the type that grips onto whatever you can while fearing for your life? Am I even talking about roller coasters anymore? No, I am not!! This metaphor is all about whether you're allowing excitement or anxiety to rule over your life? Both come from fear, but only one will serve you, while the other will undoubtedly cause unwanted stress and suffering throughout your entire life!

As an Employment Advisor, I always told my clients to

get excited about their interviews. I told them to imagine their meeting as if they were just about to see a longtime friend. I know that when I visit people that I have not seen in a while, I get so excited that I can't wait to get out of the car to spend time with them. Sometimes, I have to remind myself to put the car in park!! Choosing excitement over anxiety can quickly change the quality of your life! Let's say you're going to a job interview, and before you get there, you allow anxious thoughts to build momentum. Thoughts like, "What if I don't do well?" "What if I don't say the right thing?" "What if I don't get the job?" These types of thoughts will most likely hinder your chances of getting employed.

By choosing excitement, you're creating the opposite momentum for yourself, and even if you don't get the job, you would still feel a sense of peace within yourself. Furthermore, you might also feel happy that you did your best instead of being hard on yourself for failing. If I were an employer, I would much rather see a potential candidate demonstrate excitement over anxiety. Wouldn't you? Now, this doesn't mean that a nervous candidate wouldn't be a great fit or employee. It merely implies that the excited candidate is bringing a different type of energy to the interview. It also helps the employer determine whether or not the candidate is passionate about the opportunity.

Here's Bruce Lee's take on anxiety and excitement:
"Anxiety is the gap between the now and the then. So if you are in the now, you can't be anxious, because your excitement flows immediately into spontaneous activity."

Now, this doesn't merely apply to job search! Most of life's experiences are either met with excitement or anxiety. Using thoughts to fuel your excitement is how you'll get through most of the challenges in your life. People who get jacked about their goals achieve them with vigour, not the people who approach them with caution fuelled by anxiety. Try it for yourself right now. Pick a task or a goal that you're not too excited about. Heck, it could even be doing the dishes!!

Imagine yourself being the Dish-washing Champion of the world and that a new Challenger has come to take your title. Cue the Eye of the Tiger song by Survivor!! Get excited about the upcoming match! Envision yourself cleaning the hell out of those dishes and defending your title! Not only that but envision yourself doing it with ease and joy! Feel the sense of fulfillment you'll get after you have won in record time!! Feel it!! If you've done this with sincerity, your task will seem natural to accomplish because you were excited to take it on!! Now, try it feeling anxious! I bet you get knocked out in the first round by mommy's crock-pot!!

Every time I have approached anything in my life with anxiety, I have always felt like my best was nowhere to be found and that I mostly fell short of being great. I still did well, but I never achieved greatness. When I let go of my anxiety and open myself up to the excitement, my best is always there for me. Furthermore, the perception of what my best is changes. It's like it almost doesn't matter what outcome I end up with because I took on my task without anxiety. The result could actually be the same, but my perception has changed, and that's why letting go creates inner peace. If you get excited to do things, the odds of you doing them again increases. When it comes to life's challenges, consider choosing excitement in your life because anxiety will get in the way and hinder your progress!!

CHAPTER 21

WHAT'S YOUR INTENTION?

When I wake up in the morning, one of the first things I choose is my intention for the day. What do I mean? I'm glad you asked. What I do is ask myself what kind of day I want. Then during the day, I continuously work towards what I intended to strive for in the morning. That way life isn't happening at random but, in fact, happening because of intention. There's no such thing as random. It's all meant to show up when it does and always at the right time. Most people don't choose their intention for the day, so what they usually get is more of what happened yesterday and the day before. It's a sad cycle, and most people don't realize they're stuck in a loop, living the same day repeatedly until they die.

Many of us struggle with this, myself included. I am guilty of living the same day, without intention and purpose. I used to carry the negative thoughts of my sexual abuse into the next day all the time. Then, I wondered why things weren't getting better. I was angry, anxious, depressed, and at times suicidal. I wanted a better life but lived the same day over and over without recognizing my destructive patterns. I would think about all the terrible experiences my father put me through as a child and teenager and would often taint the experiences I was having in the present moment. I was very self-destructive and often had a clouded view of what was actually going on in life as opposed to what I thought was going on. One day, I decided to go at it, differently.

First, I decided that I would change my thought pattern right in the morning. What an excellent time to start! The thought behind my strategy was that I would beat my brain before it could start its usual thought pattern. This way, I would interrupt what my brain was about to launch instead of repeating the same emotional patterns of yesterday, which were often like riding an old roller coaster. Instead, I would tell myself that I was a happy and loving person. I decided that I would choose to be an outstanding person towards everyone I met by having an open heart...no matter what!

During my day, with my intention in mind, I willed myself towards achieving it. Let me tell you that in the beginning, I struggled with this a lot. My unhappiness habits were so ingrained in me that shaking them off would be nothing short of a miracle!! I always focused on holding my initial intention, regardless of how anyone might treat me.

The reason behind this strategy is simple and is best explained with another Dr. Wayne Dyer quote:
"How people treat you is their karma; how you react is yours."

If I didn't choose my intention right as I woke up, I missed out on the power of intention, which caused me to revert to my default state of anger, anxiety and depression. To add to this, once my intention was chosen, I continuously willed myself towards it and held onto it like a dog holding onto his favourite stick.

Second, once my thought pattern was interrupted, and I was committed to becoming a better person, I knew that choosing my thoughts more carefully would only be the beginning of my transformation. I knew that my physical state would need to match my mental state as they go hand in hand. As simple as this may sound, one of the things I did to solidify my intentions was to make my bed in the morning. I used to think that making my bed was a waste of time until I realized how much momentum is gained from this simple but meaningful act. It's like a reset button that allows you to start fresh without carrying yesterday's baggage. A new day means just that; you get a new day to give it your best, a new day to start all over!

We only have a limited time here on this planet, so it's important to make everyday count. Don't waste too many days because before you know it, they're all gone! If you don't take the only life you have seriously, you won't have a fighting chance at reaching success. So you have to get real by pulling yourself out of the hole you dug for yourself. I know it can be difficult at times, trust me, I still climb out of my hole every day! It took me many tries before my actions became healthier habits. What it boils down to is knowing what you're made of. It's pretty simple! You can intend to pursue a better life for yourself and the others around you whenever you want!!

CHAPTER 22

PHYSICAL ACTIVITIES AND YOUR MENTAL STATE

In the last chapter, "What's your intention?" I talked about how being physically and mentally healthy was something that went hand in hand. I thought of talking about another aspect of my life that has really helped me stay focused and free from harm. Working out, being active, staying fit and exercising are all sayings that mean the same thing, keeping the body moving. Even if this can mean different things to different people, it is vital to maintain a healthy lifestyle by incorporating physical activity into our daily lives. It can be from working out at the gym to running, walking, swimming and yoga. It doesn't have to be difficult or complicated.

When choosing your type of workout, it is essential to think about the goals you want to achieve. With that being said, whatever the type of exercise you're thinking of doing, please consider these points: **consistency, intensity and form**. If I were to add another principle it would be

variety. The body gets used to doing the same exercise repeatedly, which could cause your progress to plateau. The most important thing, in my opinion, is consistency. If you exercise once a week, don't expect great results. Sure once a week is a good start, but if you're serious about maintaining a healthy lifestyle, you should at least work your way up to 3 times a week. Once you've committed to your routine, focus on the intensity of your workouts. I used to put in more than an hour a day at the gym and never broke a sweat for the most part. I wasn't intense enough!! I didn't bring enough heat!! As I tweaked my routine, I realized that if I increased my intensity by decreasing the length of water breaks and overall chatting, I got better results, in less time.

I like being lean and athletic. I want to be able to play sports and be active with my family and friends while looking and feeling fit. Your goals might be different. You might want to gain muscle mass or lose those extra 20 extra pounds of fat, the type of exercise should be aligned with your goals.

Lastly, you should always be focusing on the form no matter what you do to avoid injuries to your body. You can condition your body to be strong and fit without form, but eventually, you risk injury and being injured sucks!! So basically, the workouts you do will depend on the motivation behind the results you desire. Why do you want to achieve this result? What is driving you towards this? I've been working out for about 20 years now and have worked out for different reasons throughout my life. In my twenties, it was mostly to look good at the beach...literally.

I would lift heavy weights with low repetitions. In theory, the heavier you lift, the bigger your muscles have to be to handle the load. Now that I am married and a family man, my motivation is now focused on my family; therefore, I stay fit because I want to be there for my family in a healthy state. I don't lift as heavy as I used to but have increased the number of repetitions I do per set, which gives me the athletic look I desire.

If you're just getting into exercising, choosing the type of exercise you want to do can be daunting. My advice is, keep it simple!! Don't over-complicate things by purchasing expensive pills, potions, workout gear and programs that promise outrageous results. Start by walking!! That's right!! Take a hike!! Walking is an excellent form of exercise with many benefits. Increased cardiovascular and pulmonary (heart and lung) fitness, reduced risk of heart disease and stroke, improved management of conditions such as hypertension (high blood pressure), high cholesterol, joint and muscular pain or stiffness, and diabetes are just a few benefits of walking. Walking can be done alone or in a group, and you don't need much gear. Shoes!! You'll need shoes!!

Over the last 20 years or so, I've tried P90X, calisthenics, combat training, weight lifting and a variety of stamina training such as running. All of these workouts have their advantages, but to be honest, the exercises I did in High School are pretty much the same I do now, and many of the mentioned workouts are over-kill, in my opinion. The average person doesn't need to train as a Spartan would.

The pursuit of the V-shaped waistline and chiselled 6 pack is commendable for sure. The level of commitment these people have is nothing short of remarkable. I know some people who spend 2 hours or more a day in the gym, which is one of the only ways you will achieve a Spartan-like figure. However, for the average Joe, it's completely unnecessary. Most people don't have the necessary time to dedicate themselves to the Health and Fitness Magazines' expectations.

Everyday people want to feel good and become healthier. They may want to be more flexible and not get winded when they put their shoes on, so becoming a Greek God isn't in their realm. It doesn't mean they can't do it! It merely means they do not have the desire to do it. Personally, the significant changes I have incorporated in my workouts are consistency, intensity and form. I can't stress this enough!! It doesn't matter what you do; just be consistent, be intense, maintain proper form, and the rest will fall into place.

Since High School, I haven't had the real need to modify my workouts all that much as they have always worked for me. I had always gotten great results when I followed my three principles. Again, if you're just getting into the exercise world and don't know where to start, I suggest you simply go for a 30-minute walk. Many people go right after supper with their family. It's a great way to bond with your family while maintaining physical health and is also great for instilling a routine in your daily life.

I think the best way to do all of this, especially if you're just starting out, is natural. Don't get your body used to a product that gives you a particular result, but only as long as you keep using it. I have used products like Creatine, Phosphagen HP and a variety of different protein powders and pills, which did give me results, but like I said, only if I kept using them. I'm not really against these products; in fact, I still use a Vegan based protein mix, and you would probably benefit from doing your own research before you invest your money into these products.

Another thing that I haven't talked about yet is nutrition. I'm no expert, but reading ingredients that I can't pronounce worries me and should also worry you. I don't want to say all but most packaged foods today are not good for you. They are packed with sugars and empty calories, these products are one of the major leading causes of obesity and poor nutrition. Being physically active means nothing if all you eat is junk food. Eating great food also helps your mental state as it can help clear your mind when puzzled by a problem or when you're trying to figure something out.

Dr. Mark Hyman says:
"You can't exercise your way out of a bad diet!"

My friend introduced me to working out in High School, and it truly provided me with a positive outlet and release from my experiences of being sexually abused. The fact is, I started working out at around the same time my father was arrested, and it truly saved me. I went from being suicidal to committed to fitness almost overnight. I could have easily become a coke head, but instead, working out became my drug of choice back then, and I often used it twice a day! I did it to change my thoughts because staying present when you're trying to lift heavy weights is imperative to maintaining proper form. To this day, working out and eating healthy keeps me calm, focused and driven, and I can only encourage you into pursuing the same for you and your family.

CHAPTER 23

THE THING ABOUT SEEKING ENLIGHTENMENT

I'm going to pull a line straight out of the Spiderman movie when I say that:

"With great power, comes great responsibility!"

I used this quote to make you aware that there will be a cost to your pursuit of growth and development. As much as there are benefits to pursuing growth, there is also a dark side to this pursuit. As my Wife and I chased our own version of enlightenment, I noticed something. I noticed that at the beginning of our growth centred journey, we were excited. We were so excited about the positive changes we made, which yielded great results, so we started sharing our story. We shared with friends, with family and even to a certain extent, our clients. For the most part, when we shared our story with people, they seemed enthusiastic to the point of wanting to make their own changes. I know what you're thinking "Where's the problem here?" "You've made positive changes and are now influencing others in making their own change." Well, here's where the story gets interesting.

As we promoted growth among our friends and family, something happened. A handful of our friends and family members made their own changes while the rest pretty much stayed the same. That was to be expected; not everyone was interested in the same things we were. Fair enough, I get that! Here's where shit gets really weird, as we pursued our growth, a sense of superiority developed in me. This feeling or sense grew until I started thinking that I was better than others because I was "awakened," or you could also say "woke." I started thinking, "Why aren't they taking my advice?" "Don't they know what they're doing is wrong?" "They would be so much happier if they just did what I said!"

It was like I was developing an inner voice similar to the likes of Ron Burgundy:
"I don't know how to put this, but I'm kind of a big deal!"

I was becoming very self-absorbed and pretentious. I was making videos of self-help and motivation. I was attending all these uplifting seminars and courses, but I was not following my own advice. I found myself judging my friends and family for what they ate or didn't eat because suddenly, I was a leading expert in that field. I would tell my wife, "Did you see what was in their fridge?" I had become the person who "wanted what's best for you." and not "the best for you." I was that guy!! Looking back, I realize that the reason behind my behaviour was that I was attaching too much importance to the potential outcome of those initial conversations.

I forgot that not everyone is going to want to change, but most importantly, not everyone needs to change. Some people were quite happy doing what they always did, and there's nothing wrong with that! I took myself way too seriously and took all the information gathered at these seminars and courses way too seriously! My advice...take it all with a grain of salt, as there is no one way to live a life but, in fact, many ways to live a life. What works for one may not work for the other.

Another cost associated with my pursuit of growth was the feeling of significance I got from making videos and writing blogs. I was at a party with friends, and I was listening to a couple compare the success of their videos based on how many likes they received. One said something like, "my video got this number of likes," while the other chimed in with, "well, my video got this number of likes." At that moment, I thought to myself, "Is this what I sound like?" "Do I really care that much about my online content?" "Shoot me in the head, if this is what I sound like!"

I created the videos and blogs to help myself heal from the left-over wounds of my abuse, and now I was focused on how many likes I got?? I also noticed that if my content got lots of traffic, I felt great, but if it didn't, I felt crappy. Seeking likes was one of the critical factors that made me stop creating videos and writing blogs. I wasn't able to detach myself from the outcome. I kept thinking; it shouldn't matter how many likes I get; the important thing is, am I happy while creating them? Do they bring me joy? It's like the saying, dance like nobody's watching. Now, I create stuff like nobody's going to see it, without attachment to the outcome, if you will. You can clearly see this in our Facebook Live Feeds. We do them because they're fun and a great way to start the day.

Another thing you might experience during the pursuit of growth and development is a shift in the relationships you have with friends and family. Some people get really turned off and annoyed by other people's change. Some of our friends claimed that they had nothing left in common with us because of our differences, specifically towards our eating habits. It wasn't necessarily because of what we ate but more because of how often we talked about it. Vegans love talking about their Veganism, and we were no different, "Did you know that eating meat is destroying the planet?" "Did you know that animals have feelings?" "Do you know how much water goes into the making of a burger?" and blah, blah, blah! Imagine being a Non-Vegan, and every time you meet up with Vegan friends, you get blasted for not being part of the club?! I would be turned off too!! Now that I have found a balanced diet, I get turned off by all the Vegan propaganda. It's too much! The bottom line is simple: eating meat isn't destroying the planet, eating too much meat is!!

My pursuit almost cost me my relationship with my brother because of the changes towards my religious beliefs. My brother wasn't going to invite me to his Daughter's Baptism due to my shift in beliefs. He said that he didn't think of asking me because I did not believe in God. I was astounded!! Even if my beliefs towards religion had changed, I was beside myself because I never thought something like that would happen to me! I told him that, even if I didn't believe in a traditional God, I still believed in family and supported his decision to baptize his daughter. More importantly, I still wanted us to be in each other's lives, no matter what we believed in. I also told him that it was up to me to decide whether I wanted to come to an event and that it was his job to continue to invite me, despite our different beliefs. After explaining this to him, I am happy to tell you that we have not had any issues concerning our different lifestyles since then and for that, I am grateful. In fact, I believe that we are now closer than ever!

If you are going to seek any kind of growth, you must realize that the journey belongs to you and you alone. It's great if you feel comfortable sharing your journey, that I encourage because you never know who's going to be listening. However, I genuinely believe that it should stay in the forum of sharing and not transition into preaching. People will get tired of your constant preaching and judging. Trust me, I have seen others do it and lose friends, and to a certain extent, I have done some of it myself. The same couple who counted likes said this about another person who wasn't following their advice, "she/he isn't ready yet." This famous line is as pretentious as it gets. It reminds me of the "wanting what's best for you" instead of the "wanting the best for you" line. How do you know she/he isn't ready? Ready for what exactly? How do you know what's best for that person?

I have also heard people speak of a marble jar. The marble jar is essentially a friend ranking system. The idea is, the more you hang out with a specific friend, the more marbles you put in their jar, and the opposite happens if your connection diminishes. Don't take this literally!! Don't go getting a whole bunch of jars and marbles!! It's something you do in your head! As much as I like the idea of a marble jar, I think the concept goes without saying. I mean, it's pretty obvious you are more connected with the people you see and spend time with the most. It also goes without saying that the opposite applies to the people you hang out with less. Besides, it's quite normal for friends to drift in different directions, this isn't new. What's new to me is when a person tells their friend outright that some marbles have been removed from their "friend jar" because they had to cancel plans or did not do what that person wanted. This doesn't sound like someone who is growing or enlightened to me. It seems petty and guilt-driven. I mean, how childish can a person get? This is not what flow is. When a person is in flow, they don't use these kinds of tactics, they don't even notice and are more prone to understanding others' lives.

From what I've seen and experienced, one of the goals of seeking growth and enlightenment is to free yourself from the Ego based mindset. This is a challenging thing to accomplish, and most people won't get there. Only a select few have been able to reach this state. A handful of souls have transcended to this state of pure being, and if you decide to pursue your own journey of growth, be mindful that there might be some downfalls on your path. Having said this, don't limit yourself!! Attend seminars, workshops and retreats that nourish your soul, spirit or essence! They are beneficial if you have growth and development in mind.

Speaking of attending seminars and workshops, please be mindful that your journey towards growth and development doesn't become a distraction or a form of entertainment for you. Don't let it become your new Netflix. If you attend seminars and workshops, consider implementing some of the teachings instead of using them as pure entertainment meant to make you feel good at that moment. This information was shared with you in hopes that you will take it to heart and use it to grow. I have been to several seminars and workshops, and at the beginning, I didn't take notes. I thought, "I can remember all of this, no problem!" I was always moved by the stories that people shared and always left seminars feeling better than I did before, but as time passed, the feeling dissipated, and my old beliefs and patterns would come creeping back into my life.

Robin Sharma on spiritual entertainment:
"Victims love entertainment; leaders love education!"

That was primarily because I did not have anything from the seminar to review or study. No notes to read and no notes to remind me of what the Speakers said. As you may have guessed, now, I always take notes. I have realized that anything can be used for entertainment purposes, but if you want growth, real growth, you have to study and implement what you learn. I still can't believe that some people don't take notes!! How do they expect to retain all those nuggets of wisdom, in hopes of applying them at a later date? Unless your memory is equivalent to a supercomputer, it's almost impossible to save all of what you heard. Even while reading this book, did you take notes? Did you highlight a few things here and there for you to revisit later? There must have been at least one "Ah-Ha!" moment that you want to implement for yourself?! When I attend a seminar or read a personal development book, my intention is always leaning towards growth and development, which is why I take notes. Get a journal and become your own Curator!! Write down notes, sayings, quotes and "Ah-Ha!" moments that have moved you. Even if you did nothing with the journal's content, it might be an excellent gift for a loved one.

Chinese Proverb on taking notes:
"The palest ink is better than the sharpest memory!"

As I restart my journey towards wellness, I have a better understanding that everyone has their journey. I will do my best not to get stuck on petty things. I will focus on being kind but assertive. I will challenge myself to focus on my shit while letting others focus on theirs. As I mentioned before, I truly believe we are all trying to do the best we can given our own personal experiences and that for me... is enough. Thank you!

ACKNOWLEDGEMENTS

Jeez! Where do I start? Thanking people who help you achieve a goal such as writing a book is very challenging. I want to make sure I thank everyone who has helped me on my journey and want to make sure I don't leave anybody, who deserves a mention, hanging.

Writing this book has been a labour of love and has taken me three years to accomplish and for that, I am grateful! This book started off as being a way to heal myself from childhood trauma and evolved into the book you have just read. I never thought I would complete it! I dreamed of finishing it but never thought I would follow through. I was stuck in my limiting beliefs! I believed that a person like me could not write a book, let alone publish it! As I worked towards breaking through my limiting beliefs, my mindset towards the whole process changed. I realized that anybody with the will to persevere, can accomplish anything. Furthermore, I realized that having people willing to help really facilitated the whole process. I though that I would have to go at it alone but realized that seeking help was a form of maturity. Some people helped me with the book itself while others helped without even knowing they did. Either way, these next few pages are dedicated to them.

I'm going to start by thanking my Aunt Sue. The day you decided to speak up instead of remaining silent changed me forever! **"Hate the sin, not the sinner!"** is one of the best quotes I have ever heard in my life!! It still permeates my soul to this day! You taught me that I would be on a path of forgiveness and that it would be critical for my own healing. Your words have taught me the importance in seeing people for who they are and not what they do and for that, I am grateful!

To my Uncle Dave. Thanks for stepping up when I needed you the most! You were the Father figure I needed when I was at my most vulnerable. The stories you shared about your personal life really left an impression on me! You taught me the importance of standing up to my demons by saying, **"Fighting isn't about winning, it's about showing people you won't be messed with!"** Because of your words, I would always fight back no matter how big my demons would get! You and Aunt Fran have always welcomed me into your home and I will never forget how you were there to help me. I will always cherish spending time with you! I love you!

To my Uncle Cart and Aunt Lou. Thank you for being among the first family members to re-welcome me into your home after so many years. You started a chain reaction that would encourage other family members to do the same and for that, I am grateful! The many weekends we spent at your house brought us closer together and I have many fond memories of our time spent there. Your willingness to hear me out when others wouldn't has touched me deeply. Thanks for everything you did to help me, I appreciate it! I love you!

To Ted and Josée. Thanks for encouraging me to write the book! Thanks for not judging me after sharing my story with you! You are great friends and I cherish our friendship very much! Over the years, we've grown together and apart but one thing remains the same, our unshakable ability to pick up where we left off! No matter how long we haven't seen each other, we always seem to leave off where we left off. That's the definition of a great friendship! I love you guys so much! You're part of my family!

To my Brother. Thanks for evolving with me! Our relationship could have gone south many times but your willingness to see things from another perspective shows your depth of character. Our friendship has really grown over the past couple of years and I am really happy to have you and your family in my life. You're my Brother but you're also one of my best friends. I feel totally comfortable being with you and love how close we've gotten. We didn't get the best childhood and yet, we managed to stay close despite what happened to us. I wish you nothing but the best! Love ya!

To my BFF John. Thanks for the warm and kind foreword. Your words were very touching and I will never forget them. I've known you since we were kids and even if we've had our ups and downs, we've always managed to stay good friends. Despite all we've been through, if I could have a second Brother, I would choose you hands-down. You were there for me when my world was flipped upside down, all those years ago, and you remained there for me ever since! You're a solid guy and I am very grateful to have you in my life! I love you!

To my Wife. Thank you for loving me for who I am. I can be a pain in the ass and yet, you continue to stick by me. Your ability to see me for who am I inside really warms my heart! I am forever grateful to have you by my side, you're my anchor!! We have built a great life together and because of you, I strive towards becoming a better person! You encouraged me to pursue the book and cheered me on as I processed some of my most difficult memories. You get me! You know what gets me going and what doesn't. We have been together for many years and I wouldn't change any of it! Because of you, we pursued growth and development together and have become better people because of it. You gave me the greatest gift a man could ask for, our Daughter! I wanted you to know that I love you very much!

To my Daughter. Thanks for challenging me when I needed to grow. I have developed many skills since becoming your Father, patience being the most important! You continuously push me towards becoming a better version of myself and I am super happy to have you in my life! I appreciate you! You bring me much joy and I am grateful for you! Watching you grow into the beautiful person you are becoming gives me hope for the future! You're an inspiration! I love you so much!

To my parents. Thank you for providing me the gift

of life! I wouldn't be here if it hadn't been for you. Even-though your encouragement felt disingenuous, you are the reason I wrote this book. I am the person I am today because of you! I wanted you to know that I forgive you your shortcomings. It's important to mention that even if we don't have a relationship, I still love you and wish you the best life. I am grateful for everything I experienced because of you, the good, the bad and the ugly!

QUOTES FROM OTHER INFLUENCERS AND AUTHORS

1. Napoleon Hill:

"A long while ago, a great warrior faced a situation which made it necessary for him to make a decision that ensured his success on the battlefield. He was about to send his armies against a powerful foe, whose men outnumbered his own. He loaded his soldiers in the boats, sailed to the enemy's country, unloaded soldiers and equipment, then gave the order to burn the ships that had carried them. Addressing his men before the first battle, he said, "you see the boats going up in smoke. That means we cannot leave these shores alive unless we win. We now have no choice. We win or we perish." They won. Every person who wins in any undertaking must be willing to burn his ships and cut all sources of retreat. Only by doing so can one be sure of maintaining that state of mind known as a burning desire to win, essential to success."

2. Viktor Frankl:

"Man does not simply exist but always decides what his existence will be, what he will become the next moment. By the same token, every human being has the freedom to change at any instant."

3. Rocky Balboa:

"It ain't about how hard you hit, it's about how hard you can get hit and keep moving forward."

4. Unknown Source:

"Better to remain silent and be thought a fool than to speak and remove all doubt."

5. Benjamin Franklin:

"Clean your finger before you point at my spots!"

6. Bob Marley:

"Who are you to judge the life I live? I know I'm not perfect, and I don't live to be, but before you start pointing fingers...make sure your hands are clean!"

7. Ralph Waldo Emerson:

"A foolish consistency is the hobgoblin of little minds!"

8.   Bruce Lee:

"Empty your mind, be formless, shapeless, like water. If you put water in a cup, it becomes the cup. You put water in a bottle, and it becomes the bottle. You put it in a teapot, and it becomes the teapot. Now water can flow, or it can crash. Be water, my friend".

9.   Lady Bird Johnson:

"Children are likely to live up to what you believe of them."

10.   Antoine de Saint-Exupéry:

"One's suffering disappears when one lets oneself go, when one yields - even to sadness."

11.   Tony Robbins:

"Rapport is Power!" "Rapport is created by a feeling of commonality."

12.   Henry Ford:

"Whether you think you can, or you think you can't – you're right!"

13.   Dr. Wayne Dyer:

"Change your thoughts, change your life!"

14.   Unknown Source:

"If you hang out with assholes long enough, you'll become one!"

15.   Jim Morrison:

"The most loving parents and relatives commit murder with smiles on their faces. They force us to destroy the person we really are: a subtle kind of murder."

16.   George Orwell:

"The essence of being human is that one does not seek perfection."

17.   Robin Sharma:

"Slow, steady progress is better than daily excuses."

18.   Dr. Wayne Dyer:

"When you have the choice between being right and being kind, choose kindness."

19.   Marianne Williamson:

"Forgiveness is a process, and it doesn't mean the person we forgive will necessarily be our friend—for a while, or ever. If you've done something awful to me or to someone I love, I don't see myself hanging out and having lunch with you anytime soon."

20. Ferris Bueller:

"Life moves pretty fast. If you don't stop and look around once in a while, you could miss it."

21. Oprah Winfrey:

"The more you celebrate your life, the more there is in life to celebrate."

22. J. R. R. Tolkien:

"All we have to decide is what to do with the time that is given us."

23. Frederick Douglass:

"It is easier to build strong children than to repair broken adults."

24. Grant Cardone:

"Money can't buy you happiness, but being broke can't either!"

25. Dr. Seuss:

"A person's a person, no matter how small!"

26. Dr. Wayne Dyer:

"Parents are not for leaning upon, but rather exist to make leaning unnecessary."

27.   Robin Sharma:

"The fears we don't face, become our limits!"

28.   Will Smith:

"Haters are the people who will broadcast your failures and whisper your success!"

29.   Steve Maraboli:

"If you fuel your journey on the opinions of others, you are going to run out of gas!"

30.   Audrey Hepburn:

"The most important thing is to enjoy your life - to be happy. It's all that matters!"

31.   Buddha:

"There is no path to happiness: happiness is the path!"

32.   Nathaniel Hawthorne:

"Happiness is not found in the things you possess, but in what you have the courage to release."

33.   Benjamin Franklin:

"Without freedom of thought there can be no such thing as wisdom; and no such thing as public liberty, without freedom of speech."

34. Bruce Lee:

"Anxiety is the gap between the now and the then. So if you are in the now, you can't be anxious, because your excitement flows immediately into spontaneous activity."

35. Dr. Wayne Dyer:

"How people treat you is their karma; how you react is yours."

36. Dr. Mark Hyman:

"You can't exercise your way out of a bad diet!"

37. Ben Parker:

"With great power, comes great responsibility!"

38. Ron Burgundy:

"I don't know how to put this, but I'm kind of a big deal!"

39. Robin Sharma:

"Victims love entertainment; leaders love education!"

40. Chinese Proverb:

"The palest ink is better than the sharpest memory!"

NOTES

Printed in the United States
By Bookmasters